Research Report
May 2011

CONSORTIUM ON CHICAGO SCHOOL RESEARCH AT THE UNIVERSITY OF CHICAGO

Passing Through Science
The Effects of Raising Graduation Requirements in Science on Course-Taking and Academic Achievement in Chicago

Nicholas Montgomery, Elaine M. Allensworth, with Macarena Correa

Acknowledgements

We would like to thank the many individuals and groups who helped make this report possible. Our colleagues at the Consortium on Chicago School Research (CCSR) at the University of Chicago provided critical feedback at each stage of the project. Our colleagues Takako Nomi at CCSR and Valerie Lee at the University of Michigan gave structure and perspective to this work in its formative stages. Analysts at CCSR provided thoughtful suggestions about analysis and findings at staff meetings. Jenny Nagaoka, Melissa Roderick, Sue Sporte, Diane Rado, and Claire Durwood provided critical feedback on the manuscript. Christopher Mazzeo and Emily Krone from our publications and outreach staff spent many hours working with us to clarify the findings and implications. Melanie LaForce and Michelle Scott conducted thorough technical reads of the final report. We are also thankful for the feedback from our Steering Committee, particularly the review and comments provided by Matt Stagner and Brian Spittle.

This study would not have been possible without the help of Chicago Public Schools (CPS). We are very grateful to CPS for providing the data that allowed us to undertake this project. A number of CPS staff members gave valuable feedback as we were doing this work. We are grateful to Michael Lach, Bret Feranchak, and Sam Dyson for their reactions to the research design and thoughtful comments about the implications. Melanie Wojtulewicz provided critical feedback on the manuscript, detailed information on the context within Chicago at the time of the policy, and access to the report of a task force studying graduation requirements.

This study was made possible by a grant from the National Science Foundation. It builds upon, and incorporates, work funded by the Institute of Education Sciences.

Table of Contents

Executive Summary 1

Introduction... 5

Chapter 1: *Research on Science Course Requirements* 9

Chapter 2: *Consequences of the Policy on Course Completion* 13

Chapter 3: *Consequences of the Policy on Science Learning*............. 21

Chapter 4: *Consequences of the Policy on High School Graduation and College Enrollment* 27

Chapter 5: *Interpretive Summary*.. 31

References 35

Appendix A: *Research Methodology*... 37

Appendix B: *Supplementary Tables*.. 42

Appendix C: *Survey Measures on Instruction*................................ 49

Endnotes 51

CONSORTIUM ON CHICAGO SCHOOL RESEARCH AT THE UNIVERSITY OF CHICAGO

Executive Summary

Many have expressed concerns that U.S. students are falling behind their peers on international assessments and have called on the United States to improve its competitiveness globally by enhancing students' knowledge and skills in technology, mathematics, and especially science. In response to these concerns, education reformers and policymakers have taken steps to increase science course-taking while states and school districts have raised the number of science classes required for a high school diploma and specified particular college-preparatory science classes to meet those requirements.

This policy approach seems, at first glance, to be a sensible solution to the problem of weak student performance in science. Existing research has shown that students who take high-level science course sequences have greater science learning gains in high school, are more likely to attend college, and perform better in college science classes than students who do not take these course sequences. However, the current research does not tell us whether requiring all students to take more, higher-level science classes will necessarily lead to improvements in student outcomes. After all, students who choose to take high-level science classes are often the most motivated and high-achieving students in their schools. And schools that offer advanced science courses to many students have developed the capacity to teach those courses and are often college-oriented in multiple ways. Therefore, we do not know whether science learning will improve when we require more science courses (1) to be completed by students who would not otherwise choose to take advanced science or (2) to be available in schools that would not otherwise offer these courses to most students.

> Though the new policy substantially changed the science courses students took, most students earned low grades in these classes, suggesting they were minimally engaged and learned little.

This report examines the effects of increasing science course-taking requirements in the Chicago Public Schools. CPS has been at the forefront of the national movement to require a college-preparatory curriculum for all high school students. In 1997, CPS mandated that all entering ninth-graders take a college-preparatory curriculum in high school, including three years of science coursework. This policy change occurred several years before many states raised their science requirements and eight years before the State of Illinois instituted a more modest increase (from one to two years). The previous CPS coursework policy required just one science credit; the new policy required students to take a minimum of the following courses: earth science or environmental science, biology or life science, and chemistry or physics.

To examine the impact of this curriculum policy change, this report compares outcomes for cohorts of students in Chicago before and after the 1997 policy was enacted. While the new requirements did lead to increased science course completion, we found little evidence of additional science learning or improved college outcomes. More specifically, the report shows the following:

The New Curriculum Policy Ended Low Expectations for Science Coursework

The new CPS course-taking requirements were very successful at increasing students' exposure to more science courses. Two years before the policy change, less than half of the students graduating from CPS high schools had passed three or more college-preparatory science courses; most graduates had not completed more than one science course. Immediately after the policy change, almost all graduates had passed at least three full-year science classes.

Prior to the implementation of the new science requirements, there were very low expectations for taking or learning science in the majority of CPS high schools. Even students with strong academic skills were unlikely to take three years of science coursework before the new policy; only half the graduates who had entered high school with strong academic records obtained three science credits, compared with all academically strong students after the policy was implemented. Virtually no students entering high school with weak academic skills took three years of science before the 1997 policy change.

Despite Large Increases in Course-Taking, There Were Few Improvements in Student Learning or Engagement in Science

Though the new policy substantially changed the science courses students took, most students earned low grades in these classes, suggesting they were minimally engaged and learned little. Five out of six CPS students averaged a C or lower in science after the policy change. Standardized science test score gains were minimal among students who earned Cs in their science courses and absent among those who received Ds. Most graduates earned a C average or lower in science, which was similar to the performance of graduates before the policy change.

For the small proportion of students with Bs and higher in science, the new course requirements did increase the amount of science that they learned. Before the new science requirements, 18 percent of all students averaged a B or higher in their science class. Only 11 percent of students completed three years of science while averaging a B or higher. With the new requirements, a slightly higher proportion of students completed three years of science with a B average or higher—increasing by four percentage points to 15 percent among all students, and from 18 percent to 29 percent among graduates. That small rise is important because it is students with Bs and higher who make significant gains in science test scores over time. Prior to the policy, many students who were earning Bs in science did not take more than two years of science coursework. The policy changed this.

The Course Requirement Structure Kept Some Students from Completing Higher-Level Science Courses

Though the new policy led many students to complete three years of science coursework, students were less likely to take both a year of chemistry and a year of physics after the policy was implemented—a combination that is common for students aspiring to college nationally. Because of practical concerns, CPS required students to complete earth or environmental science to meet one of the three course requirements under the policy. As a result, students had to take a fourth year of science to complete both chemistry and physics. Because few students took four years of science, fewer students graduated with the combination of chemistry and physics after the new policy was enacted.

Graduation Rates Declined Slightly

One common concern about increasing graduation requirements is that these changes can lead to higher dropout rates. Graduation rates did decrease within the first few cohorts subject to the new policy: They declined by four percentage points in the first year of the policy and another percentage point in the next year, after accounting for changes in the backgrounds and prior achievement of students entering CPS high schools. Three years after the policy change, however, graduation rates began recovering; the rates were almost at pre-policy levels after five years.

College Outcomes Did Not Improve

There were no improvements in college outcomes, despite large increases in students' college-preparatory coursework across multiple subjects. While students were more likely to graduate with college-preparatory credits in science, and in other subjects as well, college enrollment did not increase; moreover, those students who attended college were no more likely to stay in college for at least two years than students were prior to the policy change. In later years, college-going actually declined.

High Dropout Rates Limited the Potential Impact of New Science Requirements

In a school district where many students fail to graduate, increases in graduation requirements are likely to have limited potential impact on overall course completion. Though about 90 percent of CPS graduates completed the science courses, many students did not benefit from the new requirements simply because they dropped out before completing high school. The improvement in the percentage of students completing a three-course science sequence is modest if we consider all students who enter high school, including those students who failed to graduate. Only half of the students who started ninth grade in a CPS high school under the new policy completed three years of science coursework. Furthermore, only 15 percent of students who entered ninth grade finished high school with three years of science and a B average or higher after the policy change, if dropouts are included along with graduates.

Conclusion

Requiring college-preparatory coursework in science is a necessary first step towards ensuring that all students graduate from high school ready for college. The new CPS requirements have changed expectations around science coursework for both schools and students; prior to the policy change, neither students nor schools recognized science coursework as a central part of the high school curriculum. However, simply requiring students to be exposed to specific coursework is not enough to substantially improve learning in science. Course content matters only when students are engaged in learning that content and are earning strong grades. Therefore, policy solutions need to go beyond adding course requirements to address student engagement and the quality of classroom instruction in advanced science courses. Likewise, high schools in Chicago and elsewhere must go beyond simply meeting new graduation requirements to develop the kind of classroom instruction that can advance science learning and give students greater access to a wider range of colleges and competitive careers.

Introduction

Over the last two decades, education reformers repeatedly have argued that the United States can improve its competitiveness globally by enhancing students' knowledge and skills in math and especially science. In the 1980s, the seminal *A Nation at Risk* report advocated increasing the standard science coursework in high school to three years, along with similar increases in other core subjects.[1] More recently, the National Governors Association (NGA), ACT, and the American Diploma Project have called for increased science coursework and greater attention to student learning in the fields of Science, Technology, Engineering, and Math (STEM) as part of an overall effort to enhance the rigor of the high school curriculum.[2] The push for additional science learning reflects the widespread concern that students in the United States are underperforming on international assessments of science and math. On the 2006 Programme for International Assessment (PISA), 15-year-olds from the United States ranked thirty-sixth in the world in science proficiency.[3] As well, many technology experts bemoan the lack of college graduates with science degrees: In 2005, 15 prominent businesses formed the Tapping America's Potential (TAP) coalition to advocate for increasing "America's capacity to innovate" by increasing the number of college graduates in science, technology, and engineering, and by improving math and science coursework in high school.[4]

Policymakers have generally responded to these concerns by increasing the number and type of science courses required for high school graduation. In 2009, 21 states required all students to take four years of math and three years of science to graduate from high school.[5]

Chicago Public Schools (CPS) has been at the forefront of the national movement to enhance science course-taking among all high school students. Prior to 1997, students entering high school could complete any one science

> Chicago Public Schools has been at the forefront of the national movement to enhance science course-taking among all high school students.

course to meet the graduation requirements. Beginning with students entering high school in 1997, CPS raised the graduation requirements to three laboratory science courses. These three courses had to be in a college-preparatory sequence: (1) earth and space or environmental science, (2) biology or life science, and (3) chemistry or physics.

Despite the efforts in Chicago and nationally to institute new science course-taking requirements for all students, we still know comparatively little about the effects of such policies. While the existing research literature has shown that students who take high-level science course sequences have greater science learning gains in high school, it does not tell us whether changing course requirements per se leads to these improvements.

In an effort to tackle this question, we compared the coursework and academic outcomes of CPS students who entered high school before and after the new science policy took effect. The study is particularly relevant because of the current national interest in increasing curricular rigor at the nation's lowest-performing schools. When the new policy was implemented in 1997, just over half of CPS students who started high school in ninth grade graduated within four years. Only one-third of graduates attended a four-year college.

The Context for Science Course Policy Changes at CPS

In the years immediately preceding the policy, a combination of large grants, ideological appeals, and more rigorous college entrance requirements encouraged CPS leaders to raise high school science requirements. In 1994, the National Science Foundation (NSF) awarded CPS a five-year, $15-million grant to ensure "quality mathematics and science education for all students" in the district.[6] The Chicago Systemic Initiative (CSI), which was funded through the NSF's larger Urban Systemic Initiative, paid for improvements in K–12 CPS math and science education and pushed increases in graduation requirements above the low state requirements.[7] A 1994 essay by education historians Jeffrey Mirel and David Angus further shaped the thinking of CPS staff in regard to the science curriculum. The essay touted the benefits of increased graduation requirements for restoring racial equity and raising the overall quality of education.[8] The State of Illinois also raised the entrance requirements to three years of science for all of its public universities; thus, CPS graduates needed to increase their science coursework in order to apply to a public university in Illinois.[9]

In 1995, a science taskforce presented a report to the CPS Board of Education advocating more stringent graduation requirements. The report warned, however, that "simply changing the number of courses that students take without concomitant changes in content and methodology would be an exercise in futility."[10] The task force pushed for science instruction improvements in elementary schools to better prepare students to meet the new high school science requirements. To allow schools to prepare for the additional coursework, laboratory requirements, and staffing needs, the taskforce also recommended phasing in the requirements over three years. However, a new CPS administration decided to implement the new requirements without phasing them in, while providing each school with one new laboratory facility.

Changes in science requirements were part of a larger overall effort to increase the rigor of the high school curriculum in CPS. Under the new policy, students also were required to take specific college-preparatory sequences in math, English, and social science: a four-year college-preparatory English sequence, a three-year college-preparatory math sequence starting with algebra, and a three-year college-preparatory social science sequence. Prior to the policy change, students were required to take the same number of math, English, and social science courses, but without specifying that these had to be college-preparatory courses.

The CPS policy also provides insight into the logistical challenges of implementing a universal curriculum mandate in a district where the vast majority of students did not take a rigorous science sequence. The year prior to the new policy, only seven out of 74 CPS high schools had more than half of the student body completing three years of college preparatory science. As a result, the new mandate required myriad functional modifications, including new lab space, new coursework, and new classroom and teaching assignments. By necessity these practical considerations shaped how the policy ultimately was implemented.

Policymakers were forced to balance educational goals with institutional limitations when determining which courses students would be required to take under the new mandate. Specifically, policymakers had to reconcile their desire to provide equal access to rigorous science coursework with the reality that many would struggle in higher-level science courses such as chemistry and physics. This was of particular concern because policymakers acknowledged that many high school students had received weak science preparation in their elementary schools.[11]

Policymakers recognized that any flexibility in requirements (i.e., allowing students in different schools to take different course sequences) would likely lead to unequal access to rigorous coursework, with higher-scoring students starting in biology and lower-scoring students starting in earth or environmental science. However, they also recognized that mandating certain course sequences across all schools would strain the professional capacity of the system. Before the policy was initiated, only 53 CPS teachers were certified to teach physics, far too few to accommodate a universal physics mandate. In contrast, 116 teachers were certified to teach general science and 249 were certified to teach biology.[12] By state law, general science teachers were allowed to teach earth or environmental science, and biology teachers were allowed to teach environmental science. Therefore, requiring earth or environmental science, biology, and chemistry *or* physics was within the professional capacity of the system. Some CPS officials also argued that this broad sequence of courses would be of greater use to most students than a more specialized combination of chemistry *and* physics.

Thus, a mix of practical and pedagogical concerns led to the decision that all students should take earth or environmental science and those interested in specializing in science could complete chemistry and physics by taking a fourth year of science. The course sequencing decision and other details of implementation strongly influenced student outcomes. That is to say, the way that larger policy goals were translated at the district and school levels ultimately shaped how CPS students experienced high school science. This study, then, offers a window into the effects of implementing a universal science mandate in a large urban district. Ultimately, however, it provides evidence on the effects of a specific policy, in a specific district, at a specific moment in time.

Chapter 1

Research on Science Course Requirements

Existing research supports the decision to mandate more science courses in high school. Studies of high school curricula and course-taking have generally found that students with stronger coursework have better academic outcomes in high school and college. Completing at least two years of natural science is also considered to be the minimum qualification for college-going.[13] Prior research has not provided solid answers on the effects of *requiring* college-preparatory science, particularly in high-poverty, urban settings.

The existing research on course-taking falls into two general categories: studies of individual students who take different types of courses and studies of schools that offer or require different courses. The first type has found that students who take higher-level courses have greater achievement gains and are more likely to graduate from high school.[14] Some studies have also found that students with stronger science coursework are more likely to attend college and perform better in their introductory college science courses.[15] The second type of research has found that schools with stronger curricula for all students produce students with greater learning gains.[16] These "school-effect" studies include research examining differences between Catholic schools, which typically require all students to take a college-preparatory curriculum, and public schools that offer a range of courses (likened to a "shopping mall" curriculum in which students can pick and choose courses).[17] All of this work suggests that requiring students to take more science coursework should result in a higher level of science learning across a broader number of students.

> Prior research has not provided solid answers on the effects of requiring college-preparatory science, particularly in high-poverty, urban settings.

Despite the volume of studies linking coursework and student outcomes, the existing literature has limited applicability to a universal mandate requiring all schools to change their curricular offerings and all students to pass college-preparatory courses. Positive effects shown in prior studies stemmed in part from selection bias—stronger, more motivated students chose to take demanding courses or attend schools with a college-preparatory focus. The same selection bias may apply to schools that chose to require all students to take a college-preparatory course load without a universal mandate. Because they made the choice themselves, these schools presumably developed the capacity to teach college-preparatory courses to all students. This capacity includes hiring qualified teaching staff and working with teachers to develop instructional strategies for reaching students with diverse ability levels.[18] Indeed, a recent study that attempted to rule out this selection bias using a national dataset and a more sophisticated statistical technique did find notably smaller and less consistent effects than prior research suggested.[19] Even so, the study did not examine a policy mandate and may still have fallen short of completely removing selection bias.[20] What is more, ending remedial math and English coursework in CPS and requiring Algebra I and survey literature for all ninth-graders did not improve academic outcomes at all.[21] Thus, it is not clear that mandating specific science courses for an entire district would have the same effect as individual students choosing to take the courses, or schools choosing to offer advanced coursework in science.

How We Studied the Science Graduation Requirements Policy

CPS provides an ideal venue for studying the effects of curriculum mandates. The universal mandate to increase science course-taking across all CPS high schools and by all CPS students provided an opportunity to study the impact of course requirements without the problem of selection bias. Furthermore, because the policy was implemented more than 10 years ago, there was ample time to examine the long-term effects on several cohorts of students. CPS also provides a case-study for the effect of implementing such a policy in a particularly difficult environment, where students have low average achievement, low graduation rates, and low college enrollment rates. This challenge is compounded by the fact that very few students completed the science curriculum in the absence of the policy. To understand the effect of the policy, we compared students entering high school before and after the universal science mandate was implemented and asked the following questions:

1. **To what extent did the policy lead more students to complete a full college-preparatory science sequence?**
   - How many more full years of science coursework did students complete?
   - How many more students took high-level science courses that serve as a pipeline to selective colleges and science careers?

2. **Did students learn more science when required to take more science courses?**
   - Did students graduate with grades in their science courses that suggest they learned much science content?

3. **Were students less likely to graduate from high school when graduation requirements were raised?**

4. **Were students more likely to enroll and persist in four-year colleges?**

To address these questions, we compared the coursework and academic outcomes of cohorts of ninth-graders. Our study population includes 167,969 CPS students in 75 schools who entered ninth grade in successive classes from 1993 to 2001. Data on coursework come from students' transcript files, data on graduation and entry into high school come from administrative records, and data on college entry come from the National Student Clearinghouse. Administrative records were also used to obtain information on students' background characteristics, including race, gender, socio-economic status, mobility prior to high school, and age upon entering high school. Using the data records, we compiled the types and number of science courses taken by each student and the grades they received in these courses. We also determined whether the students graduated, whether they went to four-year colleges, and whether they stayed in a four-year college for at least two years. (See Appendix A for descriptions of the measures used for the study.)

We began our analysis by studying simple trends, such as the proportion of students who took three years of science in successive cohorts. Then, to ensure that any observed changes were not due to changes in the demographics or preparation of students entering high schools over time (e.g., from improving achievement among students leaving eighth grade) or changes in student composition in high schools, we ran statistical models to control for any changes in the types of students entering CPS high schools over time (see Appendix A for more information). Abrupt changes in student outcomes (e.g., course completion) that coincided with the policy change suggest that the changes were due to the policy.[22]

To gauge the full effect of the policy, we also created separate statistical models for two groups of students: one containing all students and the other limited to students who graduated. It is important to look at the effects of the policy on both graduates and dropouts, since the policy increased graduation requirements and therefore may have affected dropout rates. Yet, the policy specifically targeted the credentials of students who actually graduate. It was designed to make high school graduates better prepared for college and more knowledgeable about science. Thus, in this report, we mainly focus on the results from statistical models among high school graduates,[23] providing the results for all students in the main text as appropriate. (See Appendix B for all numbers for all students and graduates and for simple descriptive versus modeled statistics.)

Chapter 2

Consequences of the Policy on Course Completion

The change in graduation requirements led substantially more students to take and pass three or more full science courses (Figure 1). Among CPS students entering high school in 1993 through 1995, 35 percent of students who went on to graduate, completed three or more years of science. In the first year of the policy (1997), the percent of graduates completing three or more years of science courses more than doubled, to 86 percent, and then reached 90 percent the next year. Clearly, the graduation requirements had an immediate and substantial effect on course-taking for CPS graduates.[24]

In addition to the changes in course completion that occurred for students directly targeted by the policy, the mandate appears to have increased the opportunity for students in the cohort immediately prior to the policy (1996) to take more science. Compared to 1993 through 1995 freshman cohorts, more students in the 1996 cohort took three years of science. This is likely an indirect effect of the policy. Students in the 1996 cohort were in high school from 1996 through 1999 and thus still in high school after the new policy was implemented. As school leaders began adjusting course offerings in 1997 to comply with the new requirements—utilizing new science laboratories and potentially hiring more science teachers—students in the 1996 cohort were able to take advantage of the expanded availability of science courses.

> In the first year of the policy (1997), the percent of graduates completing three or more years of science courses more than doubled.

FIGURE 1

Years of college-preparatory science completed by CPS high school graduates

The new graduation requirements increased the amount of college-preparatory science completed by CPS graduates

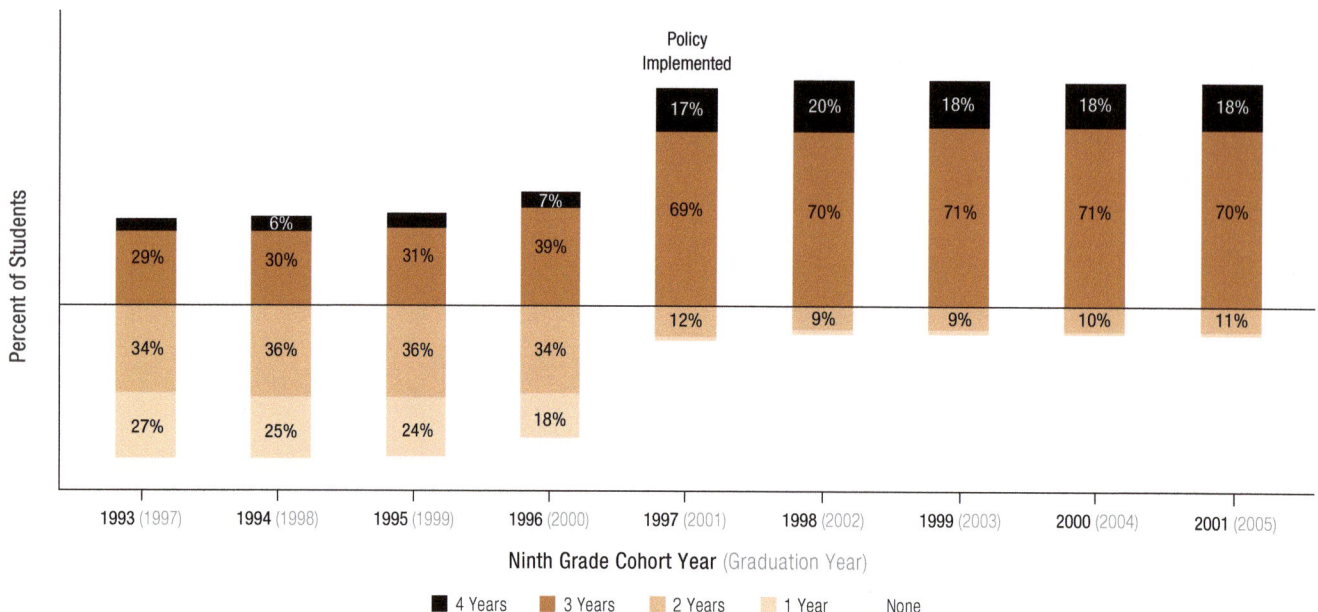

■ 4 Years   ■ 3 Years   ■ 2 Years   ■ 1 Year   None

Note: These figures control for changes in the characteristics of students entering CPS high schools over time, including students' eighth grade test scores, race, gender, and age at entry into high school (see Appendix A for more information about the statistical models).

The new policy increased science course-taking for students across a range of abilities (Figure 2). Two years prior to the policy, only half (50 percent) of students who entered high school with strong academic math skills and graduated four years later had completed three full years of science.[25] In the year prior to the policy, the availability of additional courses increased that completion rate to 56 percent for similar graduates with strong math abilities. The year the new policy was implemented the completion rate jumped to 85 percent. Each subsequent year, the completion rate increased, reaching 90 percent in 2001, which was five years after the policy was implemented.

Students entering high school with low academic math skills and graduating four years later experienced even larger improvements in science course completion. In 1995, one in four graduates (26 percent) with low incoming math skills completed three years of science. In 1996, just before the new science requirements went into place, the figure improved to one in three (34 percent). Under the new policy, the adjusted completion rate leapt to more than four out of five students (83 percent) in the first year and 88 percent in the second year. Thus, the new policy improved the transcripts of top students while simultaneously increasing equity between high- and low-ability students.

The percent of CPS graduates with four years of science on their transcripts also increased (Figure 1). Pre-policy, less than 7 percent of graduates took science for four years. Once the new science requirements were in place, an average of 18 percent of graduates took four years of science. For graduates starting high school with strong academic skills, the four-year completion rate increased from 13 percent to 28 percent. For those with weak academic skills, the rate increased from less than four percent to 12 percent. Overall, though the proportion of graduates who completed four years of science remained low, the increase under the new requirements was substantial.

Improvements in course completion also hold when we included dropouts and non-graduates in the analyses, although to a lesser degree. Raising graduation requirements has the potential to increase dropout rates by making it more difficult to meet the graduation

FIGURE 2

Adjusted percent of CPS graduates completing three years of science by incoming eighth grade test scores

The new policy increased science course completion for CPS graduates at all skill levels

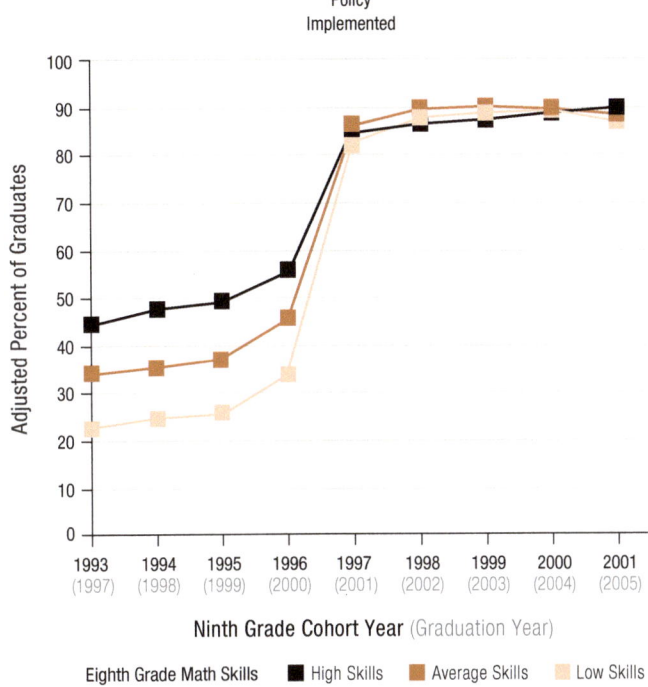

Note: Skill level is a composite of student math test scores through elementary school. Science completion rates are adjusted for changes in the characteristics of students entering CPS high schools over time, including students' eighth grade test scores, race, gender, and age at entry into high school (see Appendix A for more information). These statistics are based on first time freshmen with eighth grade test scores who enrolled in the fall of ninth grade and did not transfer out of CPS to another school district.

criteria. Thus, some of the improvements seen in science course completion among graduates could be due to a more select group of students finishing high school. However, changes in graduation rates do not explain the large changes in coursework among graduates. The increase in science coursework was dramatic even if we base our analysis on all students entering CPS high schools, including those who eventually dropped out. Pre-policy, 20 percent of students who entered CPS high schools from 1993 to 1995 (and did not transfer out) completed three years of science (Figure 3). Post-policy, about half of all students entering CPS high schools completed three years of college-preparatory science. Thus, there was a large increase in science coursework among students entering CPS high schools, even when dropouts are included in the analyses. However, almost a quarter of CPS students still dropped out in post-policy cohorts without completing any science coursework.

Despite More Years of Science, Most Graduates Did Not Complete All of the High-Level Science Courses Expected at Selective Colleges

The new science graduation requirements dramatically increased the proportion of graduates who took either chemistry or physics (Figure 4) but decreased the proportion who took both courses. Prior to the new graduation requirements (1993–95 cohorts), about two-thirds of graduates took either chemistry or physics (including those taking both chemistry and physics, and those taking advanced science). Controlling for student and school characteristics, the proportion of graduates post-policy reaching either chemistry or physics increased to 93 percent in the first year. However, the policy touched off a trend that saw fewer students taking both courses. The year before the new graduation requirements, 29 percent of graduates took both chemistry and physics—not including those students who made it to the level of advanced science. That figure dipped to 28 percent of graduates in the 1997 freshman cohort, then dropped to 20 percent for the 1998 cohort and to 12 percent for the 2001 cohort, controlling for student and school characteristics. This decline also occurred in absolute terms, that is, without adjusting for student and school characteristics.

The trend is potentially troubling. National surveys of coursework show there is a tacit hierarchy in the types of science courses that students take. Stronger students tend to take chemistry or physics, and the strongest students take both.[26] (See the sidebar on page 18, *Is There a Hierarchy of Science Courses?*) Students who take more courses in each science sub-discipline earn higher grades in introductory college courses in the same sub-discipline (e.g., biology).[27] At some institutions, college admissions officers may use this hierarchy to gauge college readiness.[28] Thus, after the policy was enacted, most CPS graduates still lacked sufficiently strong science coursework to be fully prepared for science coursework in college or for entry at very selective colleges.

The surprising post-policy decline in students taking chemistry and physics was due to the inclusion in the new requirements of earth or environmental science—

FIGURE 3

Years of college-preparatory science that CPS high school students completed, including non-graduates

CPS students left high school with more science coursework after the policy, even counting dropouts

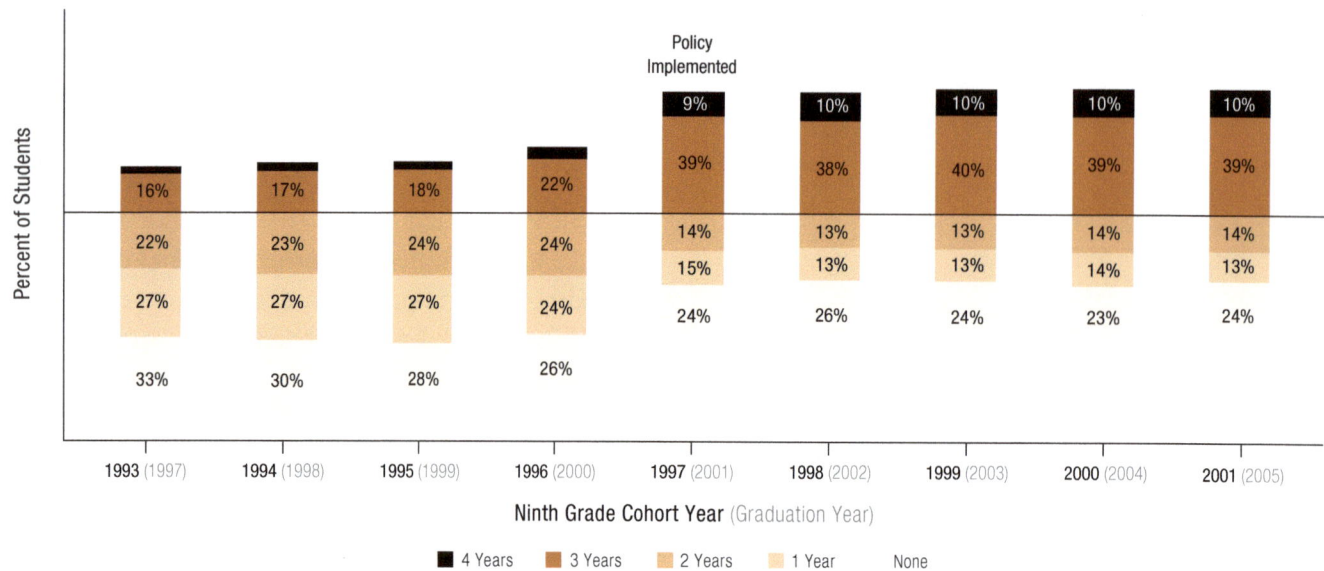

Note: These figures control for changes in the characteristics of students entering CPS high schools over time, including students' eighth grade test scores, race, gender, and age at entry into high school (see Appendix A for more information about the statistical models).

FIGURE 4

Highest level of science completed by CPS graduates

After the policy, more CPS graduates reached chemistry or physics, but fewer took both

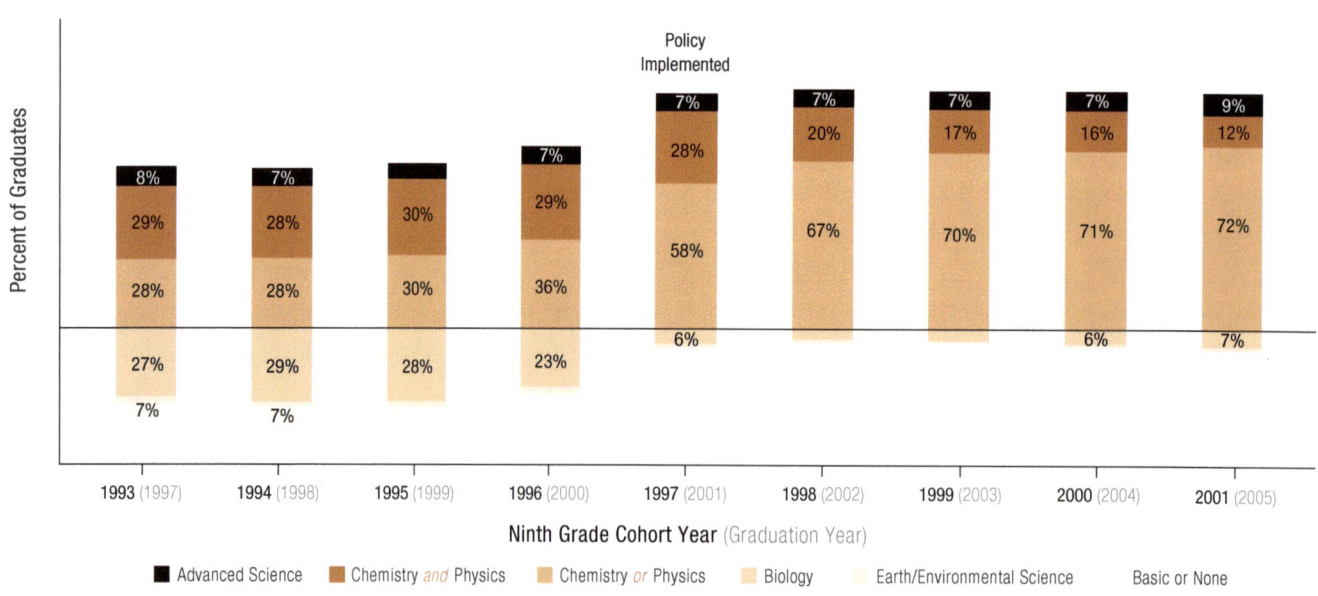

Note: The statistics control for changes in the characteristics of students entering CPS high schools over time, including students' eighth grade test scores, race, gender, and age at entry into high school (see Appendix A for more information about the statistical models).

FIGURE 5

Science course completion by CPS graduates

The policy increased earth and environmental science enrollment substantially

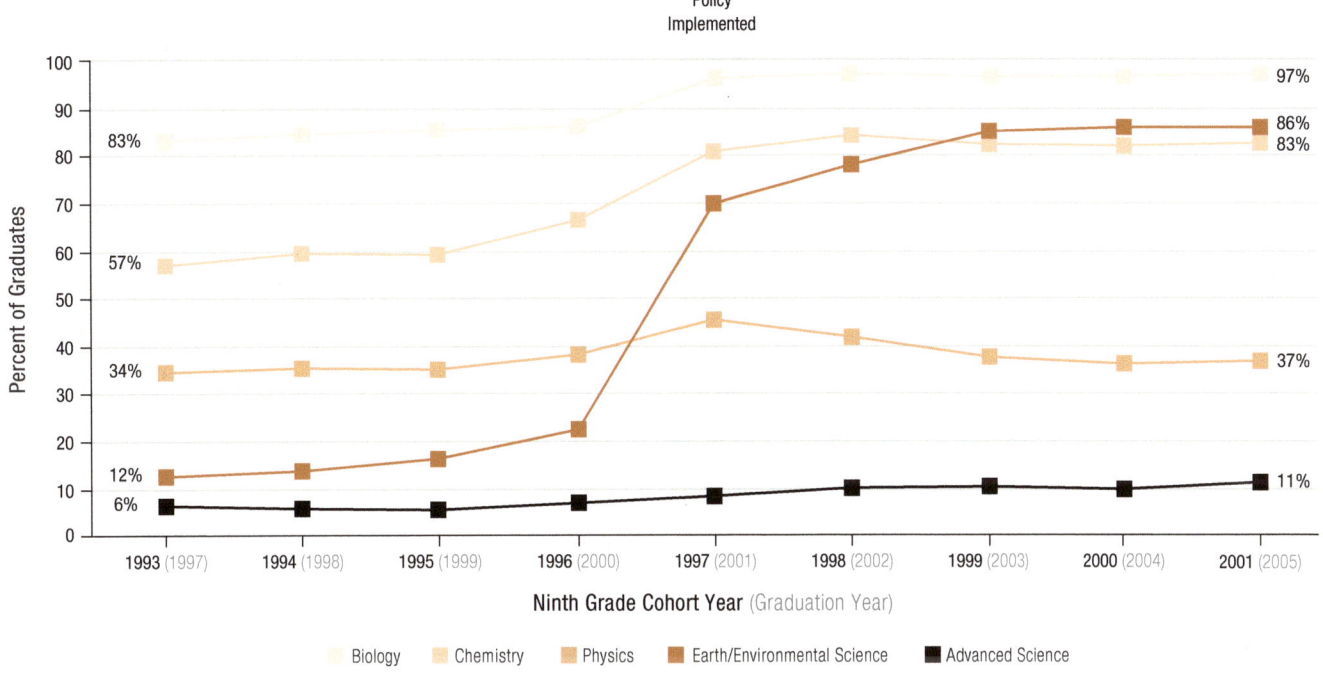

Note: Percentages do not account for changes in student demographics. The increase in advanced science completion is explained by changes in students' incoming test scores.

traditionally lower-level science courses that students rarely took pre-policy (see Figure 5). Pre-policy, just 20 percent of graduates completed earth or environmental science. Post-policy, however, the completion rate jumped to 70 percent and then reached 86 percent for the 2001 cohort.

For most students, earth and environmental science replaced biology as their entry-level science course of choice. At the outset of the policy, most ninth-graders took biology. However, the proportion of students starting high school with earth or environmental science slowly increased each year after the policy was implemented until the majority of ninth-graders enrolled in earth or environmental science instead of biology as their first science course. By starting off in earth or environmental science, most students needed to take four years of science rather than three to complete the combination of both chemistry and physics. Pre-policy, over 89 percent of graduates who completed both chemistry and physics did so with three years of science, compared to only 69 percent of graduates in the first year of the policy and 35 percent four cohorts later. Of those who did take both chemistry and physics, the majority did so with four years of science.

This is not to say that earth and environmental science courses are necessarily poor choices. Yet, specifying that these courses be taken for graduation made it less likely that students would take enough years of science to complete both chemistry and physics. This is of particular concern because there are indications that chemistry and physics are more challenging courses while, on average, students are less engaged and less challenged in earth and environmental science courses.

The new science requirements also failed to increase the percentage of students taking advanced coursework (see Figure 4). Completion of advanced science coursework (e.g., Physics II, Chemistry II, AP science courses) was unaffected by the policy change.[29] In both periods, about 7 percent of students took advanced science courses.

Chapter 2 | 17

Is There a Hierarchy of Science Courses?

Science coursework consists of a number of sub-disciplines (e.g., biology, chemistry, physics). Unlike math coursework, there is not a fixed sequence of science courses such that completion of one course necessarily indicates completion of another.[30] In science, one sub-discipline is not necessarily more difficult than the next; nor is learning from one sub-discipline a prerequisite for the next. Students who complete chemistry II have generally already taken chemistry I and know that material, but there is no guarantee that they have completed biology or physics. Nor is it the case that a biology course is necessarily more difficult or rigorous than an earth or environmental science course.

Despite the lack of a clear conceptual hierarchy between the science sub-disciplines, researchers who study curriculum have identified predominant patterns in coursework; they suggest that, in practice, schools do design their science curricula with a fairly consistent hierarchy that corresponds to students' grade level and ability.[31] Nationwide, the majority of students progress from biology to chemistry to physics. Students who take an earth or environmental science course tend to complete it in their freshman year, before they take biology; students typically complete biology before taking chemistry or physics; and students typically complete both chemistry and physics before taking advanced science at the end of high school. Thus, even though an earth or environmental science course potentially may be more rigorous than a physics course, the national patterns indicate that it is generally considered to be a low-level course at least in terms of school programming.

This hierarchy is corroborated by students' academic records; students who have the strongest academic records tend to take both chemistry and physics, while those with weak records are most likely to only take either earth or environmental science. Nationwide, most students who expect to attain a four-year bachelor's degree have taken at least chemistry or physics (69 percent of students from the graduating class of 2004); half of the students expecting to attain a four-year bachelor's degree completed both chemistry and physics or advanced science. Moreover, students who reached higher levels of the prevailing hierarchy had higher science test scores at the end of high school than students reaching lower levels (correlations between .42 and .52).[32]

The same pattern existed in CPS high schools before the new science requirements were put in place. To compare course-taking patterns among CPS students to students nationally, we classified students with a modified version of the hierarchy that was identified by researchers nationally. We placed students at the lowest level of the pipeline if they did not complete any science, completed basic science, or completed an elective science course only (e.g., astronomy, meteorology). For the next level of the pipeline, students had to complete earth or environmental science.[33] Following the course at the earth or environmental science level, students had to complete biology.[34] The next two levels are the same as the national pipeline model: chemistry or physics; then chemistry and physics. The only difference in the advanced science level is that we counted AP environmental science as an advanced science course. Prior to the new science requirements, there was a strong relationship between the pipeline identified by national researchers and college-going in CPS (Figure 6). Students only completing earth or environmental science had the lowest college-going rates, whereas students only completing biology or earth or environmental science and biology had somewhat higher college-going rates. The next level, chemistry or physics, had double the percentage of college-goers, and students at the level of chemistry and physics had double the college-going rates of students with either chemistry or physics. Students taking advanced science were the most likely to attend college. This does not mean that taking higher level courses caused students to go to college. However, it does provide further validation of the existence of an implicit hierarchy—college-oriented students (or students in more college-oriented schools) complete course combinations higher in the hierarchy.

Students also show greater increases in their science test scores if they complete science courses at the higher stages. Figure 7 shows the scores on the science portion of the 2006 ACT (taken at the end of eleventh grade). The left half of the graph shows that students only completing earth or environmental science or biology by the end of eleventh grade have the lowest test scores (15.1 and 15.4 respectively), whereas students at successive levels have higher and higher test scores (16.5, 18.4, and 21.0). This is not particularly surprising because students completing the higher levels often start with higher test scores. Yet, even after controlling for prior test scores, demographic characteristics, and school effects, students at higher levels have higher test score gains by the end of eleventh grade (shown in the right half of Figure 7). Students who started with a 15 on the pre-test taken in the fall of tenth grade and only took earth or environmental science or biology as their highest course by eleventh grade lost ground on the ACT (scoring 14.9, on average). Students passing the higher levels of science improved their test scores (scoring 15.4, 15.9, and 17 points respectively).[35]

The hierarchy of science courses is also confirmed by qualitative differences between courses at each level. CPS students taking earth or environmental science report less academic press, engagement, and

FIGURE 6

College-going rates by science sequence in 1995

College-going patterns confirm a science course hierarchy

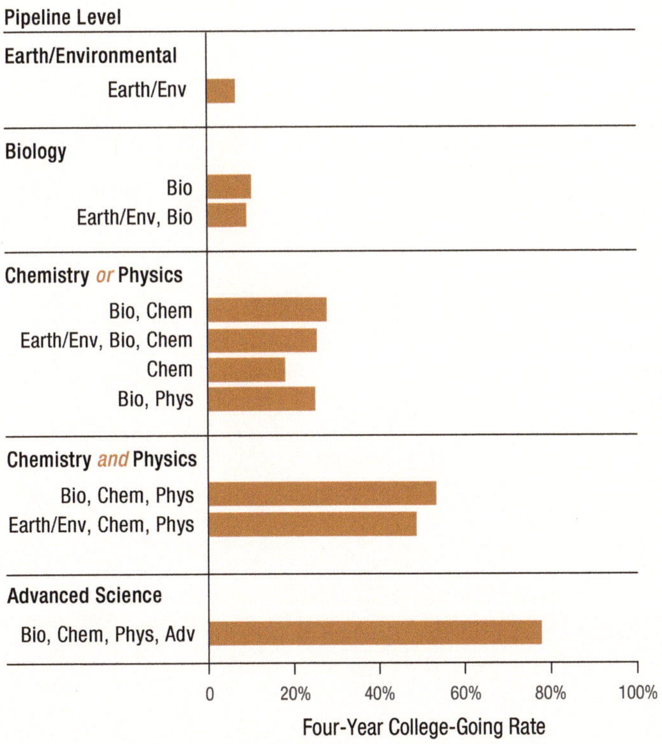

Pipeline Level
Earth/Environmental
Earth/Env
Biology
Bio
Earth/Env, Bio
Chemistry or Physics
Bio, Chem
Earth/Env, Bio, Chem
Chem
Bio, Phys
Chemistry and Physics
Bio, Chem, Phys
Earth/Env, Chem, Phys
Advanced Science
Bio, Chem, Phys, Adv
0
20%
40%
60%
80%
100%
Four-Year College-Going Rate

Note: This chart includes all students who started ninth grade in CPS in 1995 and did not transfer out, including dropouts. Several of the pipeline levels could be met with different sequences of courses; each is shown separately in this figure.

FIGURE 7

ACT science score by level of science completed by eleventh grade

Students completing higher-level science courses have higher test scores and greater gains

22
21
20
19
18
17
16
15
14
0
ACT Test Scores
No Controls
Controlling for Pre-Test and Demographics
Earth/Env
Biology
Chemistry or Physics
Chemistry and Physics
Advanced Science

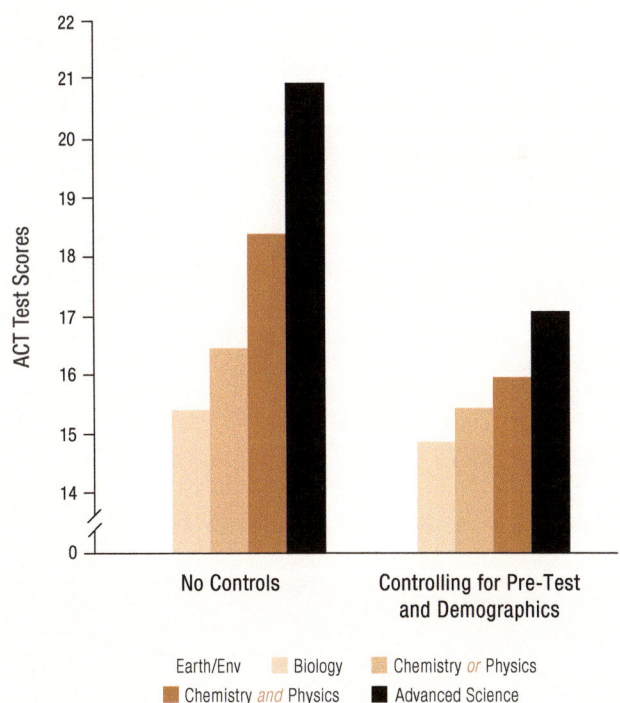

Note: Students' 2006 ACT scores controlling for tenth grade science ability, latent math ability at the end of eighth grade, and student demographics. The science scores shown here include only students taking science in their second and third year of high school and completing at least the earth or environmental science level by the end of their third year.

inquiry-based practices than students in biology, chemistry, or physics. To understand the qualitative differences between students in different science courses, we surveyed all CPS high school students in the spring of 2007. These surveys asked students a series of questions about their science course that we combined into measures of instructional climate (see Appendix C). From these reports, earth and environmental science courses in CPS seem, on average, to be less engaging and less rigorous, with less inquiry-based pedagogy than other science courses in CPS. Even when we take into account that students in earth or environmental science courses tend to have weaker academic skills than other students, or that earth or environmental science courses may be clustered in different schools, earth or environmental science courses appear to be of lower quality, on average, than other science courses taken by similar students in the same schools.

FIGURE 8

Differences in instructional environment across types of science classes, compared to biology

Biology, chemistry, and physics are more demanding and have better teaching practices than earth or environmental science

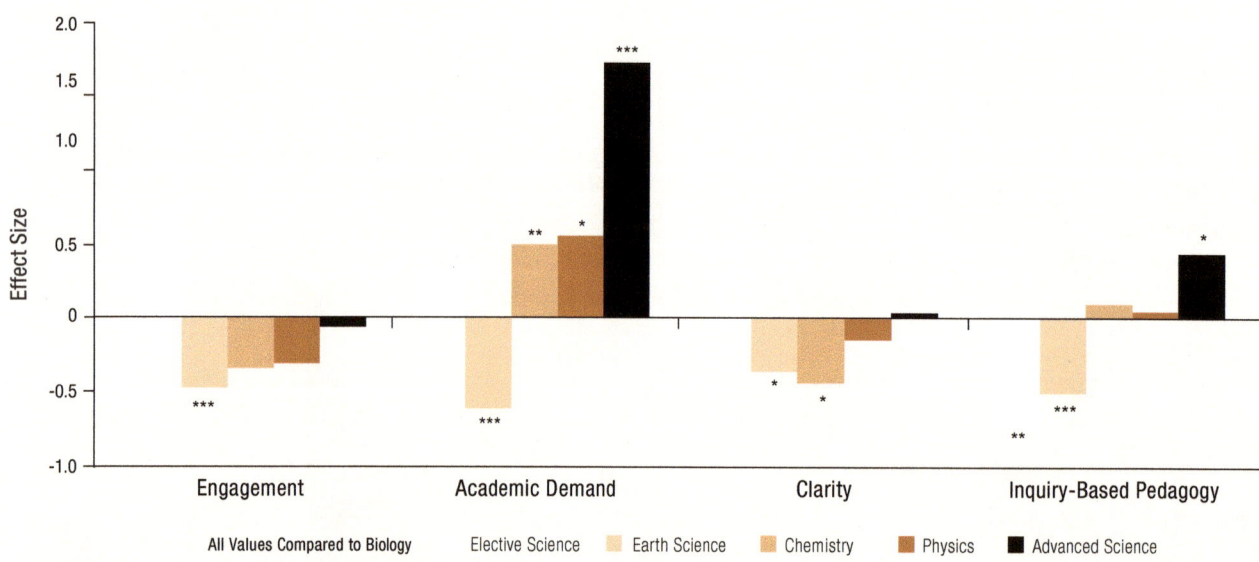

Note: Differences in instructional climate are represented in effect sizes—standard deviation units calculated in this case across classrooms. Effect sizes using standard deviations provide a means to compare outcomes for different metrics (e.g., test scores, survey measures) by converting actual values into one common metric. About 66 percent of classrooms have values on a given survey measure between 1 and -1; thus, while a classroom that is average would be at the 50th percentile, a classroom one standard deviation above the mean would be at about the 83rd percentile. In this analysis, the advanced science effect of 1.7 is extremely large.

We estimated differences between courses through three-level hierarchical models with students nested within classrooms nested within schools. At the student level, controls were included for students' EXPLORE scores at the beginning of ninth grade (regardless of which grade they were in when they took the survey), gender, race, economic status, and special education status. At the classroom level, controls were included for the classroom average incoming EXPLORE score to control for academic composition.

*$p<.05$ **$p<.01$ ***$p<.001$

Chapter 3

Consequences of the Policy on Science Learning

Though students took far more science as a result of the new requirements, there is little evidence they learned substantially more. Because pre-policy science test scores are unavailable, we use grades to gauge how much students learned. High school grades are strong predictors of college science course performance,[36] and prior research on CPS students has found that higher grades indicate both higher levels of engagement and greater learning in high school.[37] We found similar relationships between science grades and science learning. Students who earned Cs only improved their science test scores by small amounts, and there is no evidence of learning among students with Ds or Fs in science. (See the sidebar on page 24, *The Link Between Science Grades and Test Scores*.) Students needed to earn grades in the B range or higher (above 2.5 GPA) to show substantial improvements in science learning. What's more, only CPS students who earned As in science showed test score gains that were at or near expected levels, based on national norms.[38]

Most graduates completed the new science requirements with Cs and Ds—grades associated with weak to no learning. Because most post-policy graduates earned low grades in science, we might be concerned that the policy itself led to a decline in grades. There are a number of reasons such a scenario might have occurred: (1) students who would not otherwise have taken multiple years of science began taking more science courses; (2) the composition of students in science classes might have changed with the policy, with more lower-achieving students lacking appropriate academic behaviors affecting classroom climate in science classes; or (3) schools might have had

> Most graduates completed the new science requirements with Cs and Ds— grades associated with weak to no learning.

difficulty staffing the increased number of courses, resulting in lower-quality instruction.

However, the policy did not affect the distribution of science grades: They were low before the policy was enacted, and they remained low after the policy. Controlling for incoming characteristics, about one-third of post-policy graduates finished high school with a B average or higher in their science courses both pre- and post-policy, even though post-policy graduates took more science courses (Figure 9). Even when dropouts are included, the distribution of grades did not change after controlling for changes in student background. It is good news that grades did not decline with more science coursework, even though the absolute levels of performance remained low.

What's more, because the percentage of students completing three years of science increased substantially, the percentage of students completing three years of science with a B average also increased. Prior to the policy, about 19 percent of graduates completed at least three years of science with a B average or higher in those courses (Figure 10). After the policy, the figure jumped to 30 percent, an increase of 11 percentage points.

However, that increase was dwarfed by the much larger rise in the share of students completing three years of science with Cs and Ds. Between 1995 and 1997, the proportion of students completing three years of science with Cs and Ds in science increased by 38 percentage points, to 56 percent. The following year, the number increased to 61 percent. Students were taking more science courses, but earning low grades in those courses.

If dropouts are included in the analysis, the effects of the policy on science learning appear minuscule. Two years prior to the policy, 10 percent of all students who enrolled in CPS high schools completed three years of science with a B average or higher. Under the new requirements, 15 percent did so—an increase of just five percentage points. In other words, the policy likely produced a noticeable increase in science knowledge and reasoning among just 5 percent of the students entering CPS high schools. Still, this was a larger improvement than observed in any year prior to or after the policy—in no other year was there an increase of more than one percentage point in students taking three years of science with at least a B average.

FIGURE 9

Science grades for CPS graduates (includes students completing less than three years)

Increasing the number of science courses did not change the grades students received in science

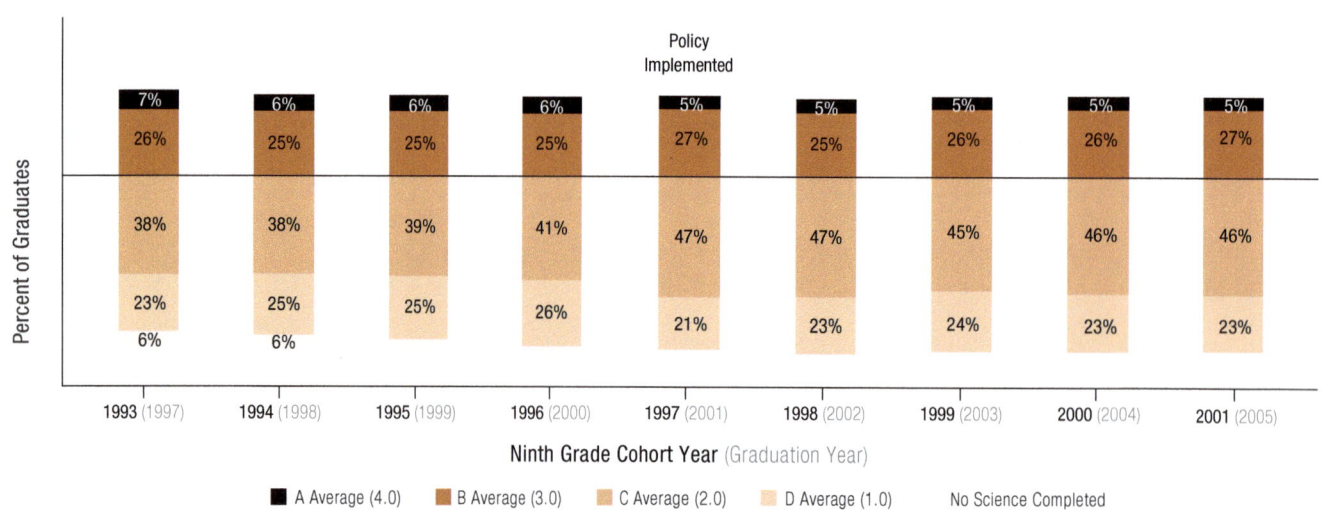

Note: Percentages control for changes in the characteristics of students entering CPS high schools over time. These characteristics include students' eighth grade test scores, race, gender, and age at entry into high school (see Appendix A for more information about the statistical models).

The slight improvements in learning resulting from more students taking three years of science might have been offset by the shift from taking chemistry and physics to taking earth or environmental science. As noted earlier, from 1997 to 2000, the proportion of students graduating after completing chemistry and physics declined by almost 12 percentage points.

This occurred because earth or environmental science became a required course. While earth or environmental courses could theoretically provide substantial opportunity to learn science, in practice they tend to have less of the qualities of instruction that are associated with high gains in science reasoning, as discussed earlier.

FIGURE 10

Science GPA of CPS graduates who completed three years of college-preparatory science

Most students completed the science sequence with Cs and Ds

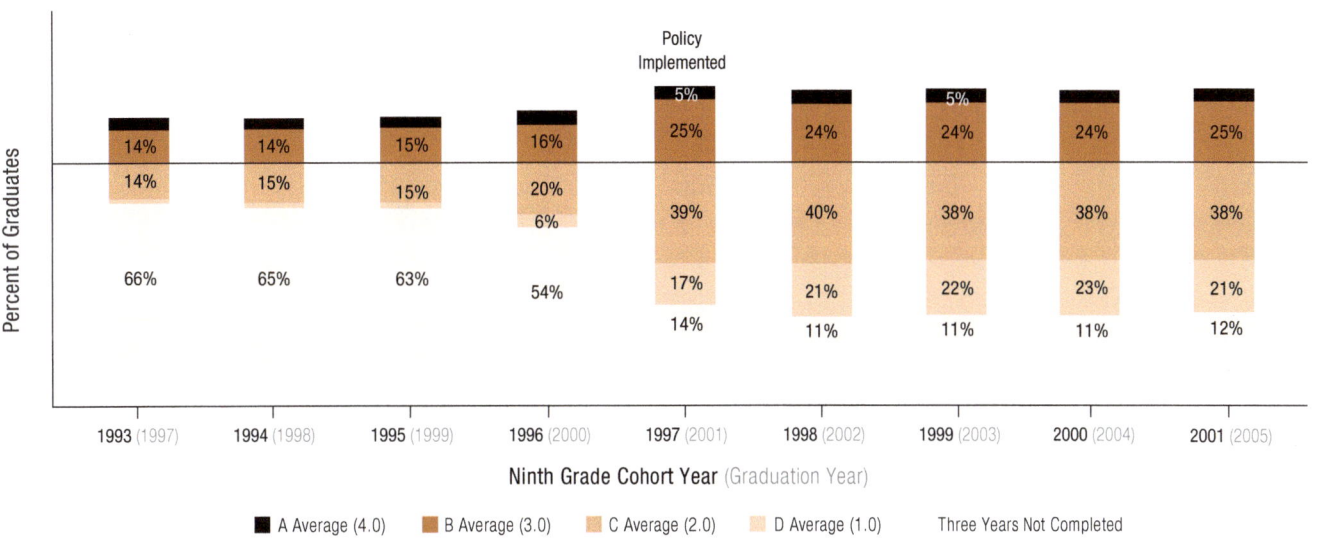

Note: The statistics control for changes in the characteristics of students entering CPS high schools over time, including students' eighth grade test scores, race, gender, and age at entry into high school (see Appendix A for more information about the statistical models and sample).

The Link Between Science Grades and Test Scores

Researchers, including those in CPS, have found that the absolute value of a grade as measured against test scores can vary widely from school to school.[39] This has led to speculation that grades are arbitrary, or at least subjective; we frequently hear that an A in one course may not be an A in another. However, prior CCSR research found strong links between grades students earn during eleventh grade, and learning as measured by test score gains in eleventh grade.[40] In this report, we show that science grades are a very strong indicator of science learning in all high school grades

Prior CCSR research found that eleventh-graders who earned higher grades showed higher test score gains in the corresponding subject. After accounting for test scores at the beginning of eleventh grade (on the PLAN), student characteristics, teacher and classroom characteristics, and school characteristics, students with higher course grades had higher scores on the ACT, taken at the end of eleventh grade. Eleventh-graders who failed or passed with Ds in their courses made no gains from the fall PLAN to the spring ACT, on average. Similarly, the increases were very small for students who received Cs. Only students who earned As or Bs had large gains from test to test, with the largest gains among students earning As. This suggests that students who fail their science courses or who pass with Ds do not learn the material; students who receive Cs learn minimal amounts. However, students who earn Bs or better truly learn in their science courses—and have the greater test score gains to show for it.

To further validate the use of science grades as indicators of learning science, we examined the link between science test score gains from the beginning of ninth grade to the beginning of tenth grade and from the beginning of tenth grade to the end of eleventh grade. Students in CPS high schools take a series of tests as part of ACT's EPAS system. Students take the EXPLORE at the beginning of ninth grade, the PLAN at the beginning of tenth grade, and the ACT at the end of eleventh grade. Each exam has a science sub-test, which we used for our analyses. Controlling for entering ninth grade EXPLORE science scores, student demographics, eighth grade math skills, the type of science courses taken, and schools' average incoming test scores, we found that ninth-graders had greater test score gains when they received higher grades.[41] As Figure 11 shows, students who received Fs in their courses made small gains (0.38 points; 0.18 SD; $p < .001$). The slight increase in scores is likely due to differences in scoring the two tests—it is unlikely that students who failed their science course learned more science. Students with Ds scored no higher than those with Fs. Students with Cs gained less than one-fourth of a point more than students with Fs (.21 points; .1 SD; $p < .05$). In contrast, students with As and Bs scored one-half a point and over three-fourths of a point higher than students who failed (.20 and .29 SD respectively).

The difference by grade was more dramatic when we examined science test gains from the tenth grade PLAN to the ACT taken at the end of eleventh grade, controlling for tenth grade PLAN science scores and student and school background characteristics. Students who averaged an F in their tenth and eleventh grade science courses lost ground on the ACT, losing over .36 points (-.12 SD; $p < .05$). Students who averaged a D in their science courses gained marginally more than those who failed their classes, but still did not make improvements over their original test score (-.09 points). Students earning a C in their courses performed better than students with lower grades, but overall made minimal gains from the PLAN to ACT. Students with Bs or As scored .64 to 1.08 points higher on the ACT respectively than students with Fs.[42] Systemwide, students earning an average of a B or higher appear to learn notably more science than those getting Cs; receiving a D average in science seems to indicate no more learning than failing the courses.

FIGURE 11

Science test score gains by science GPA

Students with higher GPAs have greater test score gains

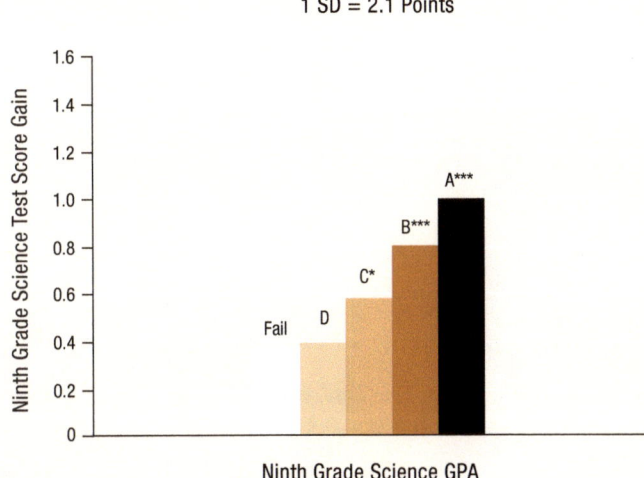

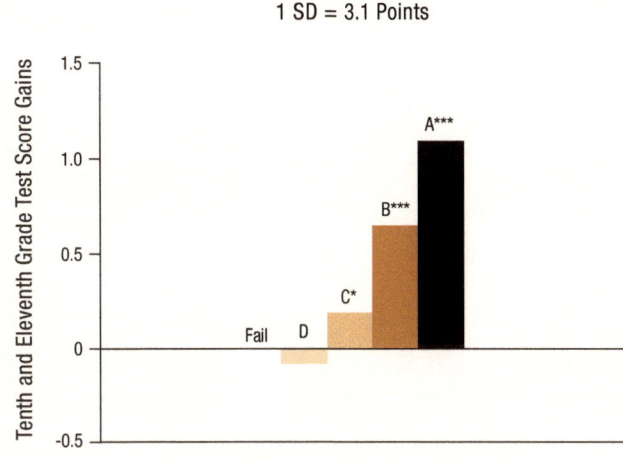

Note: Controls for ninth grade pretest, student demographics, school average ability, and science courses taken. Sample includes students from 2003 ninth grade cohort with eighth grade test scores. Ninth grade gains are based on the score change from the EXPLORE, taken in the beginning of ninth grade, to the PLAN, taken in the beginning of tenth grade.

Statistical test for difference from failure: *p<.05   **p<.01   ***p<.001

Note: Controls for ninth grade pretest, student demographics, school average ability, and science courses taken. Sample includes students from 2003 ninth grade cohort with eighth grade test scores. Tenth and eleventh grade gains are based on the score change from the PLAN, taken at the beginning of tenth grade, to the ACT, taken at the end of eleventh grade.

Statistical test for difference from failure: *p<.05   **p<.01   ***p<.001

Chapter 4

Consequences of the Policy on High School Graduation and College Enrollment

CPS raised the bar for graduating from high school by requiring students to take more courses and more difficult courses in science and in other subjects. These new requirements increased the potential for students to leave high school without a diploma. In fact, graduation rates declined with the policy, after controlling for changes in student and school characteristics.[43]

Before the new graduation policy was put in place, four- and five-year graduation rates for CPS students were increasing by small but consistent amounts annually (Figure 12). By the last pre-policy cohort, 1996, 54 percent of students graduated high school within four years and 58 percent did so within five years. Once the new graduation requirements were in place, the adjusted four-year graduation rate dipped to 50 percent (Adjusted rates need to be used because students entered CPS high schools with higher skill levels over time). Following another percentage point dip in 1998, the graduation rate then increased by two percentage points to return to the 1993 level. Five-year graduation rates followed a similar pattern, with rates dropping by three percentage points in 1997 and returning to 1993 levels in 1999.

> New requirements increased the potential for students to leave high school without a diploma. In fact, graduation rates declined with the policy.

College-Going and Retention Rates Among High School Graduates Did Not Improve

With the new graduation requirements, students graduating from CPS schools had transcripts with coursework that matched or exceeded the baseline expectations for college attendance. Despite this improvement, the new graduation requirements neither lead more CPS graduates to attend four-year colleges, nor increased college retention (measured as students staying in college for two consecutive years). Furthermore, when college-going rates are calculated with all students entering CPS high schools—including those who ended up dropping out—the college-going rate actually decreased due to the decline in graduation rates.

The new graduation requirements did not increase the likelihood of students attending a four-year college after graduation (Figure 13). Prior to the 1997 policy, when students were completing less science coursework, adjusted college-going rates for graduates were between 32 and 33 percent. In the first year following the policy, when students graduated from CPS with three years of college-preparatory science, the college-going rates dropped by a slight and not statistically significant amount, to 32 percent. In subsequent years, the rate declined further, to 30 percent and then to 29 percent by the 2000 cohort.

Given that so many students graduated with a low GPA in science, it is perhaps unsurprising that the policy shift did not improve college-going rates. Therefore, we separately examined whether students who received good grades in their science courses were more likely to attend a four-year college post-policy (adjusted for changes in student background). Our findings were disappointing. CPS graduates who averaged a B or higher (above 2.5) in their science courses, regardless of how many science courses they took, were actually less likely to attend college two years after the policy, even though they were more likely to have at least three years of science. In the pre-policy cohorts (1993 to 1996), the proportion of graduates averaging a B or higher in their science courses who went to a four-year college within

FIGURE 12

Adjusted graduation rates

The increase in graduation requirements slightly decreased graduation rates

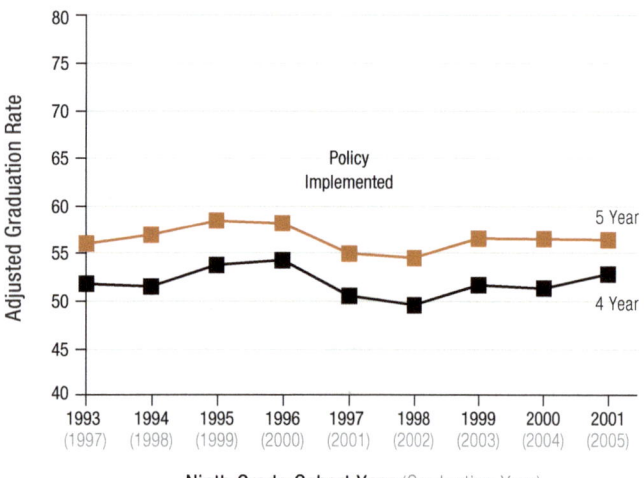

Note: Adjusted graduation rates control for changes in the characteristics of students entering CPS high schools over time, including students' eighth grade test scores, race, gender, and age at entry into high school (see Appendix A for more information about statistical models).

FIGURE 13

Adjusted college-going rates

Stronger transcripts did not drive more high school graduates to attend college

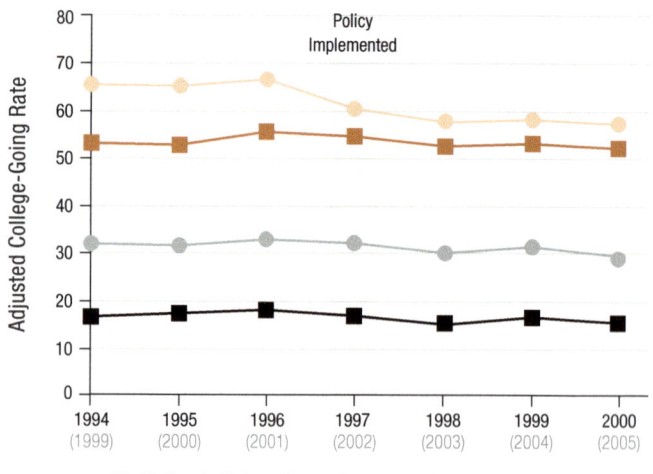

- Graduates Completeing Three Years of Science with a B or Higher
- Graduates with a B or Higher in Science
- High School Graduates
- All Students

Note: Adjusted college-going rates control for changes in the characteristics of students entering CPS high schools over time, including students' eighth grade test scores, race, gender, and age at entry into high school (see Appendix A for more information about the statistical models).

a year after high school increased from 53 percent to 56 percent. Once the graduation requirements increased, the adjusted college-going rate dropped one percentage point immediately (1997) and then dropped two percentage points in the subsequent year, leveling off at 53 percent. When we examined college-going for those students who graduated high school with at least three years of science and at least a B average, adjusted college-going rates declined even more dramatically. Two years prior to the policy, 65 percent of graduates with a B average or higher in three years of science attended college. The adjusted college-going rate increased to 66 percent just before the policy in 1996, but fell immediately to 60 percent for the first cohort required to take three years of science. It fell further, to 58 percent, with the second cohort. Again, students with strong grades and ostensibly stronger transcripts were not more likely to attend college.

Further work is needed to understand this pattern, and there are several potential explanations we plan to explore in future work. One possibility is that the switch by some high-performers from physics to earth or environmental science weakened their transcripts and ACT scores, which in turn might have led to a decline in college acceptance and scholarship receipt. In fact, by controlling for whether students took both chemistry and physics in high school, we completely explain the decline in college-going among post-policy students with grades of B or higher. However, we are reluctant to say that the act of taking physics and chemistry in and of itself increases college-going rates, as other policy effects could simultaneously have contributed to the decline in college-going.

A second possible explanation for the decline in college-going among high-achievers could be the leveling effect of the new policy. High-achievers could no longer distinguish themselves simply by taking more years of science. As a result, they might have received less attention from upper-level science teachers and less encouragement to attend college. Evidence from a prior study of this policy period found that ninth grade math and English courses became more heterogeneous (due to elimination of remedial courses), and low-ability students were more likely to be grouped with average-ability students in some schools.[44] Placing students with

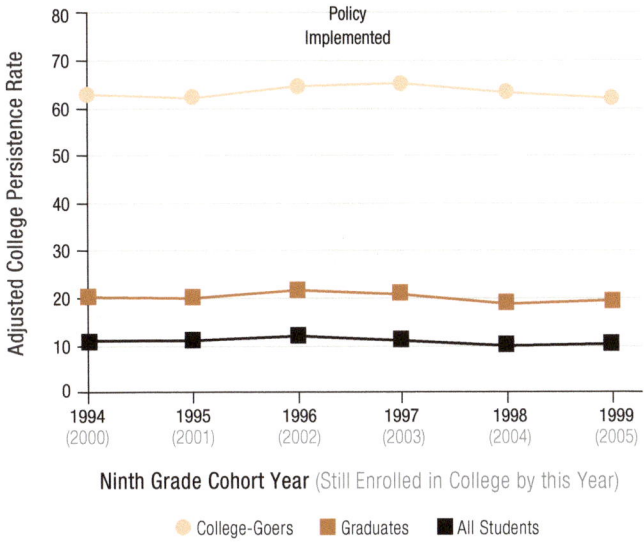

FIGURE 14
Adjusted college persistence rates

Stronger transcripts did not increase college persistence

Note: Adjusted college-going rates control for changes in the characteristics of students entering CPS high schools over time, including students' eighth grade test scores, race, gender, and age at entry into high school (see Appendix A for more information about statistical models).

little chance of going to college with students who had either a marginal or good chance of attending college might have had a negative effect on college-going. In addition, other policy changes could have affected college-going in CPS during the same time period. In particular, there was a new emphasis on the use of standardized tests for school accountability during the post-policy years. It is possible that high school counselors shifted their focus from college guidance to test preparation and administration. Further research is needed to disentangle these possible effects.

Not only were students no more likely to attend college post-policy, they also were no more likely to stay in college, despite their increased exposure to college-preparatory coursework (Figure 14). Before the increase in requirements, slightly more than 11 percent of students who entered CPS managed to graduate high school, enroll in a four-year college, and stay for two years (or transfer to another four-year college). Controlling for changes in students' background characteristics, this number dropped slightly in the first year post-policy (1997), and then fell in later years. In short, the evidence suggests that the policy may not have improved preparation for college-level coursework.

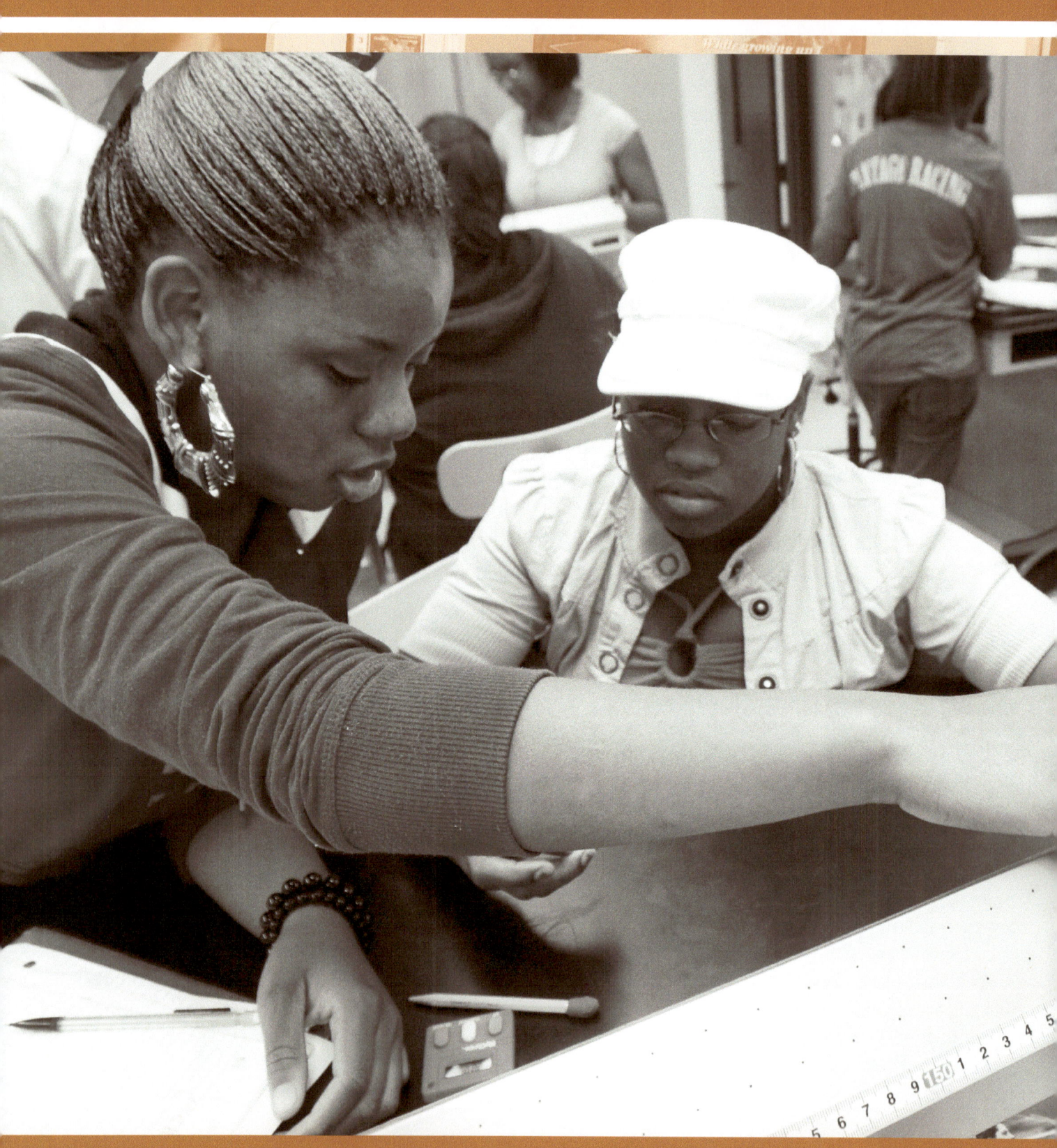

Chapter 5

Interpretive Summary

As state policymakers seek to improve the rigor of the high school curriculum and enhance student learning in mathematics and science, many have turned to increasing course requirements in these subjects. In 2009, 21 states required all students to take four years of math and a minimum of three years of science to graduate from high school; eight states were planning to do so.[45] CPS has been at the forefront of the national movement to require a college-preparatory science curriculum for all. This experience offers insights into the impact of these policies, as well as into the promise and pitfalls of implementing science coursework requirements in a challenging urban environment.

This study shows that in a district like CPS, where few students previously took more than one or two years of science, increasing graduation requirements in science can have a sizeable effect on the completion of coursework. However, it also shows that course requirements alone will not substantially increase science learning in a district with low existing performance, nor will college-preparatory course requirements necessarily increase the likelihood that students will go on to college. In short, increasing science requirements for all students has merit. But policymakers must pay particular attention to the details of implementation if students are to reap more than superficial benefits from the policy.

> **Policymakers must pay particular attention to the details of implementation if students are to reap more than superficial benefits.**

Ending Low Expectations for Science Coursework Is a Good First Step

The new policy was a resounding success in terms of increasing science course completion. Virtually all graduates took three years of science after they were required to do so, while most took only one to two years of science without those requirements. Even when we consider all students who entered CPS high schools, including those who dropped out before graduation, many more students took three years of science. It is particularly noteworthy that the policy resulted in more students taking and passing science without lowering overall science grades.

But It Is Only a First Step—Engagement Is Crucial, Too

Students took more science courses when required to do so, but low grades suggest that they were minimally engaged in these courses. The vast majority of students received Cs or lower, the same low grades they received before the policy switch. Other CCSR research has found that course failures and low grades result from students' academic behaviors—low attendance rates, poor homework completion, and little effort.[46] Raising low expectations, then, is insufficient in isolation. The content students are exposed to may matter only if educators cultivate an engaging environment and strong academic behaviors among students.

Engagement in Science Must Be Part of a Larger Effort to Keep Students in School

Because many CPS students drop out, a large number of entering ninth-graders did not complete the full complement of science courses. Simply put, graduation requirements have limited potential to impact learning in a district where nearly half of the students already fail to graduate. The good news is that the policy did not dramatically increase dropout rates, as some had feared. But neither did it fulfill the hopes of those who argue that increasing course expectations might increase student engagement and, in turn, decrease dropout rates.[47]

Policies Designed to Target Low-Performers Must Be Careful Not to Harm High-Performers

In an effort to increase equity for students with low incoming test scores, CPS designed a policy that would enable all students to take three years of science while forcing students with low and high incoming test scores to take the same set of courses. The goal was to prevent students from languishing in low-track courses. However, the policy also inadvertently made the science curriculum less demanding for top students.

The new policy required students to take courses that rank near the bottom in the traditional science hierarchy. Rarely taken before the policy, earth and environmental science courses gradually replaced biology as the entry-level science course of choice. The shift made it less likely that students would take chemistry and physics, which tend to be more challenging and to drive gains on the ACT. After the policy, students either had to skip earth or environmental science or take four years of science to take both chemistry and physics.

A number of practical constraints, including an insufficient number of certified physics and chemistry teachers, were partially responsible for the decision to require all students to take earth or environmental science, rather than both physics and chemistry. The outcome of the CPS experiment seems to corroborate other recent research showing it is extremely difficult to detrack students without also lowering the achievement of the strongest students.

More Coursework Does Not Automatically Lead to Improvements in College Outcomes

Despite large increases in students' college-preparatory coursework across multiple subjects, there was no improvement in either college enrollment or college persistence. Indeed, college-going rates actually declined post-policy among graduates with a B average or better in science. One possible explanation is that the new policy might have placed students with borderline college qualifications with students who were even less qualified, resulting in a negative peer effect. Another is the decline in physics coursework that accompanied the rise of earth or environmental science as the entry-level science course in many schools. The policy also made it more difficult for high-achievers to distinguish themselves from their peers simply by taking additional years of science. As a result, upper-level science teachers may have been less likely to single out top students and encourage their college aspirations.

Previous CCSR research has shown that college knowledge—the extent to which students have information on how to prepare and effectively participate in the college search and selection process and effective guidance and support in making decisions about college—is an important factor in shaping students' college access and success. This new study offers further evidence that no instructional reform, in isolation, can adequately address the "potholes" on the road to college faced by students; any effort to improve college enrollment must be accompanied by support structures that make students' hard work pay off.[48]

Conclusion

Recently, U.S. President Barack Obama announced a major new private-public partnership designed to boost student engagement in Science, Technology, Engineering and Math (STEM). As part of the new initiative, companies such as Intel Corp. have pledged hundreds of millions of dollars to improve STEM instruction in schools. President Obama also has made billions in federal Race to the Top funding to states partially contingent on whether they have a viable plan to improve STEM education. Underlying all of these efforts is the belief that the United States must improve science instruction to produce new scientists and remain competitive in the global economy.

Expanding and improving science education is a worthy goal, and adopting a universal college-preparatory curriculum that includes rigorous science requirements is an important first step. However, policymakers must pay attention to the lessons learned by CPS: Simply exposing more students to more science may not by itself produce a single extra science major—much less the influx of new scientists envisioned nationally.

References

Achieve, Inc. (2008)
Will Raising High School Graduation Cause More Students to Drop Out? Washington, DC: Achieve, Inc. Available online at: http://www.achieve.org/files/ImproveGradRates.pdf.

Achieve, Inc. (2009)
Closing the Expectations Gap. Washington, D.C.: Achieve, Inc. Available online at: http://www.achieve.org/files/50-state-2009.pdf.

ACT, Inc. (2004)
Crisis at the Core: Preparing All Students for College and Work. Iowa City, IA: ACT, Inc.

Allensworth, Elaine, Macarena Correa, and Steven Ponisciak (2008)
From High School to the Future: ACT Prep CPS—Too Much Too Late. Chicago, IL: Consortium on Chicago School Research.

Allensworth, Elaine M., and John Q. Easton (2007)
What Matters for Staying On-Track and Graduating in Chicago Public Schools. Chicago, IL: Consortium on Chicago School Research.

Allensworth, Elaine, Takako Nomi, Nicholas Montgomery, and Valerie E. Lee (2009)
College Preparatory Curriculum for All: Academic Consequences of Requiring Algebra and English I for Ninth Graders in Chicago. *Educational Evaluation and Policy Analysis.* 31:367–91.

American Diploma Project (2004)
Ready or Not: Creating a High School Diploma that Counts. Washington, DC: Achieve, Inc.

Attewell, Paul, and Thurston Domina (2008)
Raising the Bar: Curricular Intensity and Academic Performance. *Educational Evaluation and Policy Analysis.* 30:51–71.

Austin, Peter C., P. Grootendorst, and Geoffrey M. Anderson (2007)
A Comparison of the Ability of Different Propensity Score Models to Balance Measured Variables Between Treated and Untreated Subjects: A Monte Carlo Study. *Statistics in Medicine.* 26:734-753.

Boaler, Jo, and Megan Staples (2008)
Creating Mathematical Futures through an Equitable Teaching Approach: The Case of Railside School. *Teachers College Record.* 110:608–45.

Bryk, Anthony S., Valerie E. Lee, and Peter B. Holland (1993)
Catholic Schools and the Common Good. Cambridge, MA: Harvard University Press.

Burkam, David T., and Valerie E. Lee (2003)
Mathematics, Foreign Language, and Science Coursetaking and the NELS:88 Transcript Data. Washington, DC: National Center for Education Statistics.

Chaney, Bradford, Kenneth Burgdorf, and Nadir Atash (1997)
Influencing Achievement through High School Graduation Requirements. *Educational Evaluation and Policy Analysis.* 19:229–24.

Chicago Public Schools (2008)
Fact Sheet on the CPS EPAS Gains Metric. Chicago, IL: Chicago Public Schools.

Conley, David T. (2007)
Toward a Comprehensive Conception of College Readiness. Eugene, OR: Education Policy Improvement Center.

Dalton, Ben, Stephen J. Ingels, Jane Downing, Robert Bozick, and Jeffrey Owings (2007)
Advanced Mathematics and Science Coursetaking in the Spring High School Senior Classes of 1982, 1992, and 2004. Washington, DC: National Center for Education Statistics.

Darling-Hammond, Linda (2004)
Standards, Accountability, and School Reform. *Teachers College Record.* 106:1047–85.

Gamoran, Adam, and Matthew Weinstein (1998)
Differentiation and Opportunity in Restructured Schools. *American Journal of Education.* 106:385–145.

Greene, Jay P., and Greg Forster (2003)
Public High School Graduation and College Readiness Rates in the United States. New York, NY: Manhattan Institute for Policy Research.

Johnson, Argie, Cozette Buckney, and Paul Vallas (1994)
The Chicago Systemic Initiative (CSI), Award #9450600.

Lee, Valerie E. (2002)
Restructuring High Schools for Equity and Excellence: What Works. New York, NY: Teachers College Press.

Lee, Valerie E., and Anthony S. Bryk (1988)
Curriculum Tracking as Mediating the Social Distribution of High School Achievement. *Sociology of Education.* 61:78–94.

Lee, Valerie E., and Anthony S. Bryk (1989)
A Multilevel Model of the Social Distribution of High School Achievement. *Sociology of Education.* 62:172–92.

Mirel, Jeffrey, and David Angus (1994)
High Standards for All? The Struggle for Equality in the American High School Curriculum, 1890–1990. *American Educator.* Summer.

National Commission on Excellence in Education (1983)
A Nation at Risk: The Imperative for Educational Reform. Washington, DC: U.S. Government Printing Office.

National Governors Association Center for Best Practices (2005)
Getting It Done: Ten Steps to a State Action Agenda. Washington, DC: National Governors Association.

Oakes, Jeanne (1994)
More than Misapplied Technology: A Normative and Political Response to Hallinan on Tracking. *Sociology of Education.* 67:84–91.

Oakes, Jeanne (2005)
Keeping Track: How Schools Structure Inequality. 2nd ed. New Haven, CT: Yale University Press.

Organization for Economic Co-operation and Development (2006)
PISA 2006 Science Competencies for Tomorrow's World. Paris, France: OECD Publishing.

Powell, Arthur G., Eleanor Farrar, and David K. Cohen (1985)
The Shopping Mall High School: Winners and Losers in the Educational Marketplace. Boston, MA: Houghton Mifflin.

Price, Kelci, and Bret Feranchak (2009)
Relationship between Grades and Standardized Test Scores: Issues of Meaning and Validity. Unpublished manuscript.

Raudenbush, Stephen W., Anthony S. Bryk (2002)
Hierarchical Linear Models: Applications and Data Analysis Methods. 2nd ed. Thousand Oaks, CA: Sage Publications.

Roderick, Melissa, Jenny Nagaoka, Vanessa Coca, and Eliza Moeller (2008)
From High School to the Future: Potholes on the Road to College. Chicago, IL: Consortium on Chicago School Research.

Rosenbaum, James E. (1999)
If Tracking Is Bad, Is Detracking Better? *American Educator.* 23:24–29.

Rubin, Beth C. (2008)
Detracking in Context: How Local Constructions of Ability Complicate Equity. *Teachers College Record.* 110:646–99.

Sadler, Philip M., and Robert H. Tai (2007)
The Two High-School Pillars Supporting College Science. *Science.* 317: 457-458.

Sadler, Phillip M., and Robert H. Tai (2001)
Success in Introductory College Physics: The Role of High School Preparation. *Science Education.* 85:111–36.

Schneider, Barbara, Christopher B. Swanson, and Catherine Riegle-Crumb (1998)
Opportunities for Learning: Course Sequences and Positional Advantages. *Social Psychology of Education.* 2:25–53.

State of Illinois Board of Higher Education (1990)
Item #11: Fall 1993 Admission Requirements at Public Universities. Springfield: State of Illinois Board of Higher Education, July 10, 1990.

Tai, Robert H., Phillip M. Sadler, and John F. Loehr (2005)
Factors Influencing Success in Introductory College Chemistry. *Journal of Research in Science Teaching.* 42:987–1,012.

Tapping America's Potential (2008)
Gaining Potential, Losing Ground: Progress Report 2008. Washington, D.C.: Tapping America's Potential.

Task Force on High School Graduation Requirements in Science (1995)
Task Force Report. Chicago, IL: Chicago Public Schools.

U.S. Department of Education (1997)
Mathematics Equals Opportunity. Washington, DC: U.S. Department of Education.

Wojtulewicz, Melanie (2009)
Conversation with Melanie Wojtulewicz, former CPS Science Director.

Woodruff, David J., and Robert L. Ziomek (2004)
Differential Grading Standards among High Schools. Iowa City: ACT.

Appendix A:
Research Methodology

We determined the effects of increasing graduation requirements by comparing the academic outcomes of cohorts of students entering CPS high schools before the new requirements (pre-policy cohorts) to students entering the same high schools after the requirements were in place (post-policy cohorts). Analyses are based on the population of first time ninth-graders who were not missing data and entered non-charter CPS high schools (including all traditional, vocational, and magnet schools and academic preparatory centers) between 1993 and 2003—a total of 167,969 students in 75 schools.[49] Statistical models are used to control for changes in students' background characteristics upon entering high school (e.g., to adjust for improvements in students' math skills observed at the end of eighth grade).

Data and Indicators

Data used for analysis of policy effects included students' high school administrative records and course transcripts for four years of high school; math test scores on the Iowa Test of Basic Skills in grades 3–8; high school science test scores on the EXPLORE, PLAN, and ACT tests of the EPAS system;[50] and college enrollment and graduation data from the National Student Clearinghouse. The administrative records include students' graduation records, demographic information, and addresses. Home addresses were tied to economic information from the 2000 U.S. Census at the block group level. Transcript records include the titles and codes of all the courses that students took each semester, their grades in those courses, the schools at which they took them. We also used CPS central office electronic curriculum documentation on the meaning of course codes to determine how to classify each course taken.

Science Course-Taking

Using course codes, central office curriculum documentation, and course titles, we categorized students' science courses into specific subjects: basic science, electives, earth or environmental science, biology, chemistry, physics, advanced science,[51] and non-science. Students were coded as completing a college-preparatory science curriculum based on whether they earned full Carnegie credits in three of the five college-preparatory science subject areas (earth or environmental science, biology or life science, chemistry, physics, advanced science) within their first four years of high school. We also measured how many years of full college-preparatory science courses students completed (one or more, two or more, three or more, four or more).[52] Beyond years of coursework, we also constructed a science pipeline measure to determine the level of science course completed within the first four years of high school. Using the framework created by Burkam and Lee (2003) and modified by Dalton, Ingels, Downing, Owings, and Bozick (2007), we categorized students' high school science course-taking into six categories:

1 Basic/None
2 Earth/Environmental Science
3 Biology
4 Chemistry *or* Physics
5 Chemistry *and* Physics
6 Advanced Science

We placed students in categories based on the highest category in which they completed courses (with advanced science being the highest category). In addition to course completion measures, we compiled an un-weighted GPA of students' college-preparatory science grades across their first four years of high school (where A=4, B=3, etc.), and categorical measures of each student's grades in science in each year—D or higher, C or higher, B or higher, or A.

Student Ability

To measure students' ability levels upon entering high school, we used students' math test scores on the Iowa Tests of Basic Skills from grades 3–8. Students' raw scores on these tests were equated across forms and levels through Rasch analysis, and then further adjusted for abnormally high or low performance (e.g., a good or bad day in eighth grade) using students' growth trajectory in these six elementary school years. These adjusted "latent" scores provide a consistent measure of incoming math abilities across cohorts that is not affected by variations in difficulty across forms or different testing conditions across years.

To measure student science ability during high school, we used scores from science sub-tests on the EPAS system. As part of the system, students from the 2003 ninth grade cohort took the EXPLORE in the fall of ninth grade, the PLAN in the fall of tenth grade, and the ACT in the spring of eleventh grade. Each of these tests included a science reasoning sub-test. CPS first administered the ACT to juniors in the spring of 2001; these students were mostly from the 1998 ninth grade cohort. As a result, we could not use the ACT to measure student science ability prior to the 1997 science policy.

Student Socio-Economic Status

We used several variables to measure differences in socio-economic status. One was just a simple indicator based on participation in the federal subsidized school lunch program; students were receiving free lunch, reduced-price lunch, or no subsidized lunch. However, because the majority of CPS students receive free lunch, this indicator does not satisfactorily identify CPS students with different economic backgrounds. Therefore, we also used data from the 2000 U.S. Census at the block group level to classify the economic status and poverty level in students' residential block group. This provides a much more nuanced indicator because there are 2,450 block groups in which CPS students live. We measured the concentration of poverty within a census block as the percent of males over 18 employed one or more weeks during the year and the percent of families above the poverty line. After inversing the two percentages, we took the log of each, standardized the results, and averaged them. To calculate social status of a census block, we used census information on residents' job type and education; we then averaged the two. For the former, we used the log of the percent of persons 16 years or older who were managers or executives. For the latter, we used the mean level of education among persons over 18. We standardized both before averaging.

Analytic Strategy

One of the shortcomings of prior research is that studies often compare cross-sections of schools with many course-taking requirements to schools with few. Such comparisons do not adequately address questions of how a *universal mandate* in which *all* schools are required to change their curricular offerings, and *all* students are required to take college-preparatory classes would affect student outcomes. Without a universal mandate, schools that had developed the capacity to enroll all students in college-preparatory coursework may have been different than other schools in unmeasured ways; for example, they may have had a culture that was committed to diversity in education or a mission to prepare all students for college. These unmeasured school differences could have affected students' outcomes, rather than the differences in coursework. Similarly, studies that compare students who complete strong curricula to students who complete weaker curricula do not account for unobservable differences between students.

To overcome the weaknesses of prior research, we used an interrupted time series design, comparing successive cohorts of students entering CPS in the same high schools pre- and post-policy. This shows what happened to similar students in *the same schools* under different curricular policies. Using this design, we looked for changes in student outcomes (e.g., likelihood of completing three years of college-preparatory science), as well as changes in the trends in those outcomes (e.g., an acceleration or deceleration in the changing likelihood of completing three years of college-preparatory science).

A simple interrupted time series would solely provide information on the changes in CPS as a whole; it would not account for changes over time in students incoming abilities, demographics, or differences between schools. To account for those concerns, we used statistical models to control for student background and school differences.

Models

We specify models with students nested within cohorts nested within schools. The hierarchical models take into account the grouped nature of the data; that is, students in a particular cohort are more similar to each other than students in other cohorts, and students within a series of cohorts inside one school are more similar to each other than students in a series of cohorts in another school. These models allow us to compare cohorts of students entering each school post-policy to students with the same background characteristics entering the same school pre-policy. Below is an example of how we specified the models at each level. We used these models for analyzing grades, years of college-preparatory science, level of science attained, high school graduation, college enrollment, and college-persistence. For illustration, we discuss the interpretation of the models for predicting the probability of completing science.

Student-Level Model

To model the probability of students completing science with a B or higher, we used hierarchical generalized linear models.[53] At the student level, the model consisted of an intercept, a series of covariates, and a random effect to account for variation that occurred among students within cohorts:

$$\text{Probability}(Y_{ijk}=1|B) = P_{ijk}$$

$$\text{Log}(P_{ijk}/1-P_{ijk})]_{ijk} = \pi_{0jk} + \sum_{p=1}^{P}\left(\pi_{pjk} * X_{pijk}\right) + e_{ijk}$$

The covariates (X) that we included were:
- Student eighth grade latent math ability
- Eighth grade latent math ability squared
- Race/ethnicity dummy variables (White, Latino, Asian; African American was the omitted category)
- Free/reduced price lunch dummy variables (reduced lunch, no lunch; free lunch was the omitted category)

- Gender
- Special education status
- Age variables (young for grade dummy variable, old for grade dummy variable, months older than expected)
- Mobility variables (moved once in the last three years, moved twice in the last three years)
- Social and economic status variables (poverty in residential neighborhood, economic status in residential neighborhood)

We centered all student variables around the 1996 average so that the intercept represented the probability of completing the science sequence for students with background characteristics that were typical for students entering high school in 1996, the last pre-policy year.

Cohort-Level Model

At the cohort level, we included a dummy variable to represent every cohort. To control for any changes in the composition of students entering schools over time, we also included a time-varying covariate that measured the difference between the current cohort's average math ability and the 1996 average for the school. Only the intercept was allowed to vary randomly at the school level. The coefficients on the cohort variables (βs) show the difference in the percentage of students in each school attaining the science sequence compared to students entering that school in 1996, controlling for differences in their background characteristics. The intercept of the cohort equation, β_{00}, represents the 1996 cohort.

$\pi_0 = \beta_{00} + \beta_{01}(1993 \text{ cohort}) + \beta_{02}(1994 \text{ cohort}) + \beta_{03}(1995 \text{ cohort}) + \beta_{04}(1997 \text{ cohort}) + \beta_{05}(1998 \text{ cohort}) + \beta_{06}(1999 \text{ cohort}) + \beta_{07}(2000 \text{ cohort}) + \beta_{08}(2001 \text{ cohort}) + \beta_{09}(\text{Difference in average math ability from 1996}) + r_{jk}$

All other π are fixed at levels 2 and 3, without predictors.

School-Level Model

At the school level, we controlled for the school average math ability. Other possible covariates were tested (racial composition, school type—magnet, vocational, regular, school size), but were not significant once average ability was controlled so we did not include them in the final model for parsimony.[54]

$\beta_{00} = \gamma_{000} + \gamma_{001}(\text{School average math ability}) + u_k$
$\beta_{09} = \gamma_{090} + \gamma_{091}(\text{School average math ability})$

The remaining coefficients (cohort dummy variables) were fixed at the school level because we were interested only in district-wide averages.

Model for the Link Between Grades and Test Scores

To model the relationship between grades and test scores, we used two-level linear models with students from the 2003 ninth grade cohort nested inside schools. At the student level, we controlled for the same variables as in the models described, grand mean centered, plus several additional variables. In addition to latent math ability, we controlled for pre-test scores (EXPLORE or PLAN), using dummy variables for scores 10 and lower, and for all values between 11 and 32 that had observations (PLAN and EXPLORE score of 15 was the omitted category). We also controlled for the science GPA in college-preparatory courses during the time period measured with the gains, using dummy variables for each grade (A, B, C, D; failure omitted). We did not center GPA, so the intercept represented an average PLAN score for a student with an F average in the grade tested; dummy variables for grades discerned the difference in gains for students with higher grades in their science course. To remove school compositional effects we controlled for school-average ninth grade EXPLORE score at the school level on the intercept, on each PLAN score, and on the course grade variables. Only the intercept and the dummy variable representing an A in science were allowed to vary randomly across schools; the latter was allowed to vary because gains for very high-achieving students varied significantly by school.

Appendix B:
Supplementary Tables

TABLE 1

Number of Students in Analyses

First Time Freshmen Cohort	Total	Graduates	College-Goers
1993	20,117	10,252	n/a
1994	20,422	10,461	3,314
1995	19,561	10,247	3,197
1996	18,206	9,867	3,239
1997	16,813	8,864	3,103
1998	18,380	10,010	3,413
1999	17,805	10,198	3,468
2000	18,269	10,423	3,359
2001	18,396	10,824	n/a

TABLE 2
Number of Years of College-Preparatory Science Courses by Cohort

Graduates		Adjusted (Percent)					Actual (Percent)				
First Time Freshmen Cohort		0	1	2	3	4	0	1	2	3	4
Pre-Policy	1993	4.8	26.8	34.2	29.0	5.1	4.8	26.6	33.5	29.6	5.5
	1994	4.3	24.8	35.8	29.7	5.5	3.8	22.5	36.6	31.2	6.0
	1995	3.0	24.4	36.0	31.2	5.5	3.2	23.3	35.9	31.7	5.8
	1996	2.0	18.3	34.1	38.8	6.9	2.0	18.3	34.1	38.8	6.9
Post-Policy	1997	0.3	1.3	12.0	69.4	16.9	0.2	0.8	7.9	76.6	14.5
	1998	0.4	1.0	9.1	69.5	19.9	0.2	0.5	4.9	74.4	20.0
	1999	0.3	1.0	9.4	71.5	17.9	0.2	0.6	5.2	74.6	19.5
	2000	0.2	0.6	10.1	71.2	18.0	0.1	0.5	5.5	74.8	19.1
	2001	0.1	0.5	10.9	70.4	18.0	0.1	0.3	5.7	72.3	21.6

All Students		Adjusted (Percent)					Actual (Percent)				
First Time Freshmen Cohort		0	1	2	3	4	0	1	2	3	4
Pre-Policy	1993	32.8	27.1	21.6	15.9	2.7	33.6	27.1	20.9	15.6	2.8
	1994	30.4	26.6	23.4	16.7	2.9	30.6	26.1	23.3	16.9	3.1
	1995	28.3	27.2	24.0	17.6	3.0	29.3	26.9	23.1	17.5	3.1
	1996	25.9	24.0	24.1	22.2	3.8	25.9	24.0	24.1	22.2	3.8
Post-Policy	1997	23.6	14.5	14.0	39.1	8.9	20.6	13.1	12.6	45.9	7.8
	1998	25.9	13.4	12.5	37.9	10.4	19.9	11.2	11.3	46.4	11.2
	1999	24.0	13.1	13.3	39.9	9.7	18.0	11.2	11.2	48.2	11.4
	2000	22.9	13.6	14.3	39.4	9.8	17.0	11.5	11.5	48.8	11.2
	2001	24.0	12.6	13.9	39.5	9.9	17.4	10.7	11.6	47.5	12.9

Note: Adjusted numbers control for differences in students' background characteristics and entering test scores across the cohorts, compared to students entering high school in 1996. (See Appendix A for details on the statistical models.)

Appendix B

TABLE 3
Highest Level of Science Completed by Cohort

Graduates												
	Adjusted (Percent)						**Actual** (Percent)					
First Time Freshmen Cohort	None	Earth Science	Biology	Chem. or Physics	Chem. and Physics	Advanced Science	None	Earth Science	Biology	Chem. or Physics	Chem. and Physics	Advanced Science
1993	7.0	2.0	27.1	27.6	28.6	7.7	6.8	2.3	28.3	32.2	24.1	6.3
1994	6.6	2.2	28.5	27.8	28.4	6.5	5.7	1.9	27.1	33.6	25.5	6.2
1995	4.6	2.4	28.2	29.6	29.9	5.3	4.5	2.9	27.4	33.8	26.0	5.4
1996	2.9	2.5	22.8	35.6	29.4	6.9	2.9	2.5	22.8	35.6	29.4	6.9
Post-Policy												
1997	0.3	0.4	6.0	57.8	28.2	7.2	0.2	0.3	4.3	59.0	27.9	8.2
1998	0.4	0.3	4.4	67.1	20.4	7.4	0.3	0.2	2.6	62.5	24.7	9.7
1999	0.3	0.3	5.0	70.1	16.9	7.4	0.3	0.2	3.1	67.0	19.3	10.2
2000	0.2	0.2	5.8	70.7	15.7	7.4	0.2	0.1	3.7	68.9	17.5	9.5
2001	0.2	0.2	6.5	72.1	11.9	9.2	0.1	0.1	4.0	66.2	18.8	10.7

All Students												
	Adjusted (Percent)						**Actual** (Percent)					
First Time Freshmen Cohort	None	Earth Science	Biology	Chem. or Physics	Chem. and Physics	Advanced Science	None	Earth Science	Biology	Chem. or Physics	Chem. and Physics	Advanced Science
1993	35.2	2.6	25.2	17.2	15.6	4.1	36.1	2.8	25.6	19.6	12.7	3.2
1994	33.0	2.8	26.4	18.8	15.3	3.6	33.4	2.8	26.2	20.6	13.6	3.4
1995	30.4	3.6	26.6	19.6	16.8	2.9	31.6	3.8	26.5	21.0	14.2	2.9
1996	27.5	3.6	24.5	23.9	16.7	3.8	27.5	3.6	24.5	23.9	16.7	3.8
Post-Policy												
1997	23.4	4.1	16.6	37.3	14.9	3.8	20.7	3.6	15.7	39.9	15.7	4.4
1998	25.6	4.2	15.5	40.7	10.1	3.9	20.0	3.6	13.6	43.1	14.2	5.4
1999	23.8	4.8	15.8	42.9	8.7	4.0	18.1	4.1	13.5	46.6	11.7	5.9
2000	22.6	5.0	17.2	43.3	7.9	4.0	17.2	4.2	14.4	48.0	10.6	5.5
2001	23.7	5.0	16.1	44.0	6.1	5.0	17.4	4.2	13.8	46.5	11.6	6.4

Note: Adjusted numbers control for differences in students' background characteristics and entering test scores across the cohorts, compared to students entering high school in 1996. (See Appendix A for details on the statistical models.)

TABLE 4

GPA in All Science Courses by Cohort

Graduates

First Time Freshmen Cohort		Adjusted (Percent)					Actual (Percent)				
		None/Fail	D	C	B	A	None/Fail	D	C	B	A
Pre-Policy	1993	6.0	23.3	37.7	25.6	7.4	5.8	26.9	38.0	23.4	6.0
	1994	5.5	24.8	38.0	25.4	6.2	4.7	26.7	38.5	24.4	5.7
	1995	4.4	25.1	39.0	25.4	6.1	4.1	26.8	38.6	24.8	5.7
	1996	2.7	26.2	40.5	24.7	5.9	2.7	26.2	40.5	24.7	5.9
Post-Policy	1997	0.3	20.9	47.2	26.6	4.9	0.2	19.8	46.6	27.7	5.6
	1998	0.4	22.7	46.8	25.1	5.0	0.3	19.9	46.0	27.4	6.4
	1999	0.4	23.7	44.5	26.3	5.1	0.3	20.9	44.0	28.7	6.1
	2000	0.2	22.8	45.8	26.4	4.8	0.2	19.4	45.4	29.0	6.0
	2001	0.2	22.6	45.5	26.7	4.9	0.2	19.2	44.9	29.6	6.1

All Students

First Time Freshmen Cohort		Adjusted (Percent)					Actual (Percent)				
		None/Fail	D	C	B	A	None/Fail	D	C	B	A
Pre-Policy	1993	32.2	25.6	24.1	14.2	4.0	33.3	26.9	23.8	12.8	3.2
	1994	30.5	27.4	24.6	14.1	3.5	31.0	27.9	24.6	13.4	3.1
	1995	28.2	27.9	25.9	14.6	3.4	29.5	28.5	25.1	13.9	3.1
	1996	26.3	29.2	27.0	14.2	3.3	26.3	29.2	27.0	14.2	3.3
Post-Policy	1997	23.0	30.5	29.7	14.3	2.6	20.4	30.5	30.6	15.4	3.0
	1998	25.2	30.0	29.0	13.2	2.6	19.7	29.8	31.3	15.7	3.5
	1999	23.2	30.7	28.9	14.4	2.7	17.7	30.3	31.3	17.1	3.6
	2000	21.9	31.3	29.6	14.6	2.6	16.4	30.3	32.3	17.4	3.5
	2001	23.3	30.0	29.2	14.9	2.7	16.8	29.6	31.7	18.2	3.7

Note: These figures represent the percentage of students with grades of A (above 3.5), B (above 2.5 to 3.5), C (above 1.5 to 2.5), etc. in their science courses in each cohort, regardless of which science courses students took or how many science courses they took. Students who took no science courses are included with students in the none/failed category. Adjusted numbers control for differences in students' background characteristics and entering test scores across the cohorts, compared to students entering high school in 1996 (see Appendix A for details on the statistical models).

TABLE 5

Science GPA for Three Years of College-Preparatory Science

Graduates		Adjusted (Percent)					Actual (Percent)				
First Time Freshmen Cohort		None/Fail	D	C	B	A	None/Fail	D	C	B	A
Pre-Policy	1993	65.8	1.8	13.9	13.9	4.5	64.9	3.7	14.5	13.0	3.9
	1994	64.8	2.4	15.0	14.0	3.7	62.9	3.7	15.9	14.0	3.7
	1995	63.3	3.0	15.4	14.6	3.7	62.5	3.6	15.5	14.7	3.7
	1996	54.4	5.6	19.9	15.8	4.3	54.4	5.6	19.9	15.8	4.3
Post-Policy	1997	13.7	16.7	39.4	25.4	4.9	8.9	15.8	43.2	26.6	5.4
	1998	10.5	21.1	39.8	23.7	4.9	5.7	17.5	43.9	26.7	6.2
	1999	10.7	22.3	37.8	24.4	4.9	6.0	18.2	41.9	27.9	6.0
	2000	10.8	22.7	38.0	23.9	4.6	6.1	16.9	42.9	28.2	5.9
	2001	11.6	21.0	38.2	24.5	4.7	6.2	16.3	42.5	29.0	6.0

All Students		Adjusted (Percent)					Actual (Percent)				
First Time Freshmen Cohort		None/Fail	D	C	B	A	None/Fail	D	C	B	A
Pre-Policy	1993	81.5	1.5	7.4	7.3	2.4	81.6	2.1	7.7	6.7	2.0
	1994	80.4	2.1	8.2	7.3	2.0	80.0	2.3	8.6	7.2	1.9
	1995	79.5	2.1	8.5	7.8	2.0	79.4	2.3	8.6	7.8	2.0
	1996	74.0	3.6	11.4	8.7	2.3	74.0	3.6	11.4	8.7	2.3
Post-Policy	1997	52.1	9.5	22.6	13.3	2.5	46.3	11.2	25.2	14.4	2.9
	1998	51.8	11.1	22.4	12.3	2.5	42.4	12.8	26.4	14.9	3.4
	1999	50.5	11.6	22.1	13.1	2.6	40.4	13.4	26.5	16.2	3.5
	2000	50.8	12.0	21.9	12.8	2.4	40.1	13.1	27.0	16.4	3.4
	2001	50.6	11.1	22.4	13.4	2.5	39.6	12.3	27.2	17.4	3.5

Note: These figures represent the percentage of students with grades of A (above 3.5), B (above 2.5 to 3.5), C (above 1.5 to 2.5), etc. in three years of college-preparatory science courses. Students who did not complete three years of college-preparatory science courses are included in the "none/fail" category. Adjusted numbers control for differences in students' background characteristics and entering test scores across the cohorts, compared to students entering high school in 1996 (see Appendix A for details on the statistical models).

TABLE 6
Graduation Rates

First Time Freshmen Cohort		Adjusted Graduation Rates (Percent)		Actual Graduation Rates (Percent)	
		Four Year	Five Year	Four Year	Five Year
Pre-Policy	1993	51.7	55.8	51.0	55.3
	1994	51.5	56.9	51.2	56.3
	1995	53.8	58.2	52.4	56.7
	1996	54.2	58.0	54.2	58.0
Post-Policy	1997	50.2	54.8	52.7	57.1
	1998	49.3	54.3	54.5	59.4
	1999	51.6	56.3	57.3	61.5
	2000	51.3	56.5	57.1	61.6
	2001	52.8	56.4	58.8	61.9

Note: Adjusted graduation rates control for changes in the characteristics of students entering CPS high schools over time, including students' eighth grade test scores, race, gender, and age at entry into high school (see Appendix A for more information).

TABLE 7
College-Going Rates

First Time Freshmen Cohort		Adjusted College-Going Rates (Percent)				Actual College-Going Rates (Percent)			
		All Students	High School Grads	Grads with B or Higher in Science	Grads Completing Science Curriculum with B or Higher	All Students	High School Grads	Grads with B or Higher in Science	Grads Completing Science Curriculum with B or Higher
Pre-Policy	1994	16.9	31.8	53.0	65.4	16.6	31.7	52.2	65.4
	1995	17.2	31.6	52.7	65.2	16.7	31.2	53.0	65.6
	1996	18.1	32.8	55.5	66.4	18.1	32.8	55.5	66.4
Post-Policy	1997	16.7	32.2	54.6	60.1	18.9	35.0	56.7	57.5
	1998	15.4	30.1	52.7	57.6	19.1	34.1	54.4	54.8
	1999	16.4	31.0	53.3	57.9	19.8	34.0	54.0	54.5
	2000	15.6	29.4	52.4	57.2	18.8	32.2	52.6	53.1

Note: Adjusted graduation rates control for changes in the characteristics of students entering CPS high schools over time, including students' eighth grade test scores, race, gender, and age at entry into high school (see Appendix A for more information).

TABLE 8
College Persistence Rates

First Time Ninth Grade Cohort		Adjusted College Persistence Rates (Percent)			Actual College Retention Rates (Percent)		
		All Students	High School Graduates	College-Goers	All Students	High School Graduates	College-Goers
Pre-Policy	1994	10.5	20.0	62.9	10.1	19.4	61.2
	1995	10.7	19.6	62.4	10.3	19.5	62.4
	1996	11.6	21.2	64.6	11.6	21.2	64.6
Post-Policy	1997	10.7	20.9	65.1	12.2	22.9	65.5
	1998	9.7	19.0	63.3	12.4	22.3	65.5
	1999	9.8	18.8	62.0	12.6	21.9	64.3

Note: Adjusted college persistence rates control for changes in the characteristics of students entering CPS high schools over time, including students' eighth grade test scores, race, gender, and age at entry into high school (see Appendix A for more information).

Appendix C:
Survey Measures on Instruction

The analysis of classroom climate is based on responses to surveys given in the spring of 2007 to students in grades 9–12 in CPS high schools: 115 high schools (84 percent) participated in the survey with sufficient response rates to be included in the analysis; the average response rates within those schools was 70.1 percent in grades 9–10 (39,945 students), 61.7 percent in grade 11 (13,920 students), and 57.5 percent in grade 12 (10, 502 students). Only students who took science answered questions about science pedagogy, for a sample of 32,315 students. Other indicators of the classroom environment (engagement, press, clarity, personalism) were based on a further sub-sample of students; surveys asked students to answer questions about the class they have just before lunch, which was science for only a sub-set of 7,119 students.

Academic Engagement (engg)

How much do you agree with the following statements about this class (Strongly Disagree, Disagree, Agree, Strongly Agree):

1. I usually look forward to this class
2. I work hard to do my best in this class
3. Sometimes I get so interested in my work, I don't want to stop
4. I often count the minutes until class ends
5. The topics we are studying are interesting and challenging
6. I am usually bored in this class

Course Clarity (clar)

How much do you agree with the following statements about this class (Strongly Disagree, Disagree, Agree, Strongly Agree):

1. It is clear what I need to do to get a good grade
2. The work we do in class is good preparation for the tests
3. I learn a lot from feedback on my work
4. The homework assignments help me learn the course material

Academic Press (pres)

How much do you agree with the following statements about this class (Strongly Disagree, Disagree, Agree, Strongly Agree):

1. This class makes me really think
2. My teacher expects me to do my best all the time
3. My teacher expects everyone to work hard

In this class, how often (Never, Once in a While, Most of the Time, All the Time):

4. Do you find the work difficult
5. Are you challenged
6. Does the teacher ask difficult questions on tests
7. Does the teacher ask difficult questions in class
8. Do you have to work hard to do well

Classroom Personalism (perc)

How much do you agree with the following statements about the teacher for this class (Strongly Disagree, Disagree, Agree, Strongly Agree):

1. Notices if I have trouble learning something
2. Will help me improve my work if I do poorly on an assignment
3. Really listens to what I have to say
4. Believes I can do well in school
5. Is willing to give extra help on schoolwork if I need it
6. Helps me catch up if I am behind

Inquiry-Based Science Pedagogy (scie)

In your science class this year, how often do you do the following (Never, Once or Twice a Semester, Once or Twice a Month, Once or Twice a Week, Almost Every Day):

1. Use laboratory equipment or specimens
2. Write lab reports
3. Generate your own hypothesis
4. Take notes on your observations of an experiment or nature
5. Use evidence/data to support an argument or hypothesis
6. Find information from graphs and tables
7. Do library/internet research to learn what scientists have discovered on a topic

Endnotes

Introduction

1. National Commission on Excellence in Education (1983).
2. National Governors Association Center for Best Practices (2005); ACT, Inc. (2004); American Diploma Project (2004), National Governors Association (2007).
3. Organization for Economic Co-operation and Development (2006).
4. Tapping America's Potential (2008).
5. Achieve, Inc. (2009).
6. Johnson, Buckney, and Vallas (1994), abstract.
7. Wojtulewicz (2009).
8. The Mirel and Angus essay was included in a 1995 CPS task force report on science requirements (Mirel and Angus [1994]).
9. The only exception is the University of Illinois. Due to an additional foreign language requirement, the University of Illinois campuses only require two years of science. Biology, chemistry, and physics were explicitly preferred. State of Illinois Board of Higher Education (1990).
10. Task Force on High School Graduation Requirements in Science (1995), preface.
11. Wojtulewicz (2009).
12. Some teachers hold certificates in more than one sub-discipline.

Chapter 1

13. Greene and Forster (2003).
14. Chaney, Burgdorf, and Atash (1997); Schneider, Swanson, and Riegle-Crumb (1998).
15. U.S. Department of Education (1997); Sadler and Tai (2001); Tai, Sadler, and Loehr (2005).
16. Bryk, Lee, and Holland (1993); Lee and Bryk (1989); Lee and Bryk (1988); Lee (2002).
17. Powell, Farrar, and Cohen (1985).
18. Several studies have shown a number of problems and difficulties accompanied by efforts to detrack classrooms (Gamoran and Weinstein [1998]; Oakes [1994]; Rosenbaum [1999]). Although some schools have successfully detracked classrooms and improved instruction for low-ability students (Boaler and Staples [2008]; Oakes [2005]; Rubin [2008]), characteristics of such schools seem to be exceptional, with a shared belief in diversity among staff, successful professional development that led teachers to use inclusive pedagogical practices, and additional supports for struggling students.
19. Attewell and Domina (2008).
20. The Attewell and Domina (2008) study used propensity score matching to determine the likelihood of students selecting to take stronger academic curricula. The authors then compared test scores for students with the same likelihood of taking the curricula to each other and compared test scores for those who took the stronger curricula to test scores for those who did not. The propensity model can be weakened by inadequately modeling student likelihood of taking the curricula. In this case, the model only used seven characteristics of students and explained just under 50 percent of the variance in student coursework. If there are unmeasured characteristics of the students that are related to taking the curricula and student test scores, the estimate of the outcome (test scores) could be incorrect (Austin, Grootendorst, and Anderson [2007]).
21. Allensworth, Nomi, Montgomery, and Lee (2009).
22. This is called an interrupted time series design (see Appendix A for more information). While this is generally considered a strong research design, the weakness of this method is that other policies that occurred simultaneously to the one being studied could potentially affect the interpretation of policy effects. Because CPS is a large, complex, and reform oriented system, there are multiple policies being implemented over time. However, abrupt changes in student outcomes that correspond exactly with the year of policy implementation suggest that the changes were likely due to the policy.
23. We define graduates as those students receiving a diploma in four years.

Chapter 2

24. In this instance, we are comfortable making a causal statement. In the CPS context—particularly after controlling for student demographics, test scores, and school compositional changes—there is no reason for such a dramatic shift to happen in the year of the policy. Moreover, the policy says that all graduates must take three years of science in order to receive a diploma, so it is hardly surprising that virtually all graduates do, in fact, take three years of science.
25. Students with strong academic math skills are those who have latent math scores one standard deviation above the 1996 mean. Students with low academic math skills are those with latent math scores one standard deviation below the 1996 mean. See Appendix A for more information on the latent math scores.
26. Burkam and Lee (2003); Dalton et al. (2007).
27. Sadler and Tai (2007).
28. Students with more advanced coursework, particularly AP or IB courses, have access to more selective schools than peers with less advanced coursework (Roderick, Nagaoka, Coca, and Moeller [2008]).

29 There were small increases in students completing advanced science post-policy; however, these increases were not statistically significant after controlling for student characteristics. Instead, they were due to changes in students' skill levels at entry into high school. Later cohorts had higher eighth grade achievement, on average, than earlier cohorts. Among students entering high school with similar skill levels pre- and post-policy, there was no increase in advanced science coursework. Only in 2001 was the rate of advanced science completion statistically higher than 1996, with a 2.3 percentage point increase.

30 Math sequences, by and large, move students from algebra to geometry to algebra II to pre-calculus to calculus. Thus, it is generally correct to assume that students who have completed pre-calculus have learned the material in algebra I, even without seeing it on a student's transcript.

31 Burkam and Lee (2003); Dalton et al. (2007).

32 Dalton et al. (2007), p. 7.

33 In the national hierarchy of science courses, earth science is considered a basic science and environmental science is considered a secondary or elective science. However, because the CPS requirements treated earth and environmental science equivalently, we grouped them together as earth or environmental courses.

34 There are several different courses at the biology level nationally that do not qualify for this category in CPS high schools because CPS treats them as electives.

35 Some school characteristics explain these differences. With additional controls for the average ninth grade test score in the school as well as random differences between schools, the relationship between pipeline level and test score gains is reduced somewhat, but still holds the same pattern. This is additional evidence that some schools choose to structure the course sequences for their students differently, and it is the characteristics of those schools that produce stronger gains (in this case, lower average incoming test scores). Moreover, CPS students who have only completed earth or environmental science or biology likely failed courses or were otherwise behind in their coursework. Yet, this confirms a national portrait that stronger students tend to complete courses higher in the science hierarchy.

Chapter 3

36 Sadler and Tai (2001); Sadler and Tai (2007).

37 Allensworth, Correa, and Ponisciak (2008); Allensworth and Easton (2007).

38 Chicago Public Schools (2008).

39 Woodruff and Ziomek (2004); Price and Feranchak (2009).

40 Allensworth, Correa, and Ponisciak (2008).

41 Though the relationship between grades and test scores does suggest that science GPA is a good indicator of student learning, there is still a large degree of variation in test score gains. The standard deviation of gains was 2.10 at the student level, after controlling for pre-test scores.

42 Controlling for all of the student and school level characteristics without grades, we were able to explain 89 percent and 84 percent of student level variation in test score gains, respectively, for gains in grades 9–10 and in grades 10–11. Adding grades explained an additional 1 percent of variance in each set of gains.

Chapter 4

43 The science policy was part of a larger increase in graduation requirements increases across multiple subjects. The credit increase in science and social science, as well as the specification of college-preparatory courses in math and English, combined to make a larger policy that temporarily affected graduation rates. Because the science policy is inextricably linked with the changes in graduation requirements in other subjects, we are unable to identify whether some specific subject-area components affected graduation rates more than others.

44 Allensworth, Nomi, Montgomery, and Lee (2009).

Chapter 5

45 Achieve (2009).

46 Allensworth and Easton (2007).

47 Achieve (2008).

48 Roderick, Nagaoka, Coca, and Moeller (2008).

Appendix A

49 At the time of publication, charter schools in Chicago did not share electronic student transcript records with the CPS central office. As a result, we have no information on their course-taking patterns. Student missing data (e.g., elementary test scores) were excluded from all analyses.

50 Information on the EPAS testing system (which includes the EXPLORE, PLAN, and ACT) is available at http://act.org/epas/.

51 Advanced science courses include advanced biology, chemistry II, physics II, and AP science courses.

52 Though students generally only took one unit of science each year, some earned multiple credits over the span of a year. We treated two credits in different subjects (e.g., biology, chemistry) as two years of college-preparatory science, regardless of the year in which they were taken.

53 Raudenbush and Bryk (2002).

54 For the analyses of graduation and post-secondary outcomes, we also controlled for magnet schools and whether the school was one of the 33 schools with an African American population above 85 percent. These were significant predictors for only these outcomes.

About the Authors

Nicholas Montgomery

Nicholas Montgomery is a Senior Research Analyst at the Consortium on Chicago School Research (CCSR). Nicholas holds a master's degree in Education Research and Policy from the University of Michigan's School of Education and a bachelor's degree in Computer Science from Brown University. Currently, Nicholas is a leader of the Data and Practice Collaborative, a new effort to deliver coherent data reports to schools based on CCSR's research and to work with networks of schools to improve the reports and their usage. Nicholas is also researching the effects of high school curriculum policy changes at CPS.

Elaine M. Allensworth

Elaine Allensworth is the Interim Co-Executive Director of CCSR. She has published widely on the structural factors that affect high school students' educational attainment, particularly the factors that affect graduation and dropout rates. Elaine is currently leading a mixed-methods study of the transition to high school, as well as several studies on the effects of rigorous curricular reforms on instruction, grades, test scores, high school graduation, and college attendance. She holds a PhD in Sociology and an MA in Sociology and Urban Studies from Michigan State University, and she formerly worked as a high school Spanish and science teacher.

This report reflects the interpretation of the authors. Although CCSR's Steering Committee provided technical advice and reviewed earlier versions, no formal endorsement by these individuals, organizations, or the full Consortium should be assumed.

This report was produced by CCSR's publications and communications staff.

Editing by Ann Lindner
Graphic Design by Jeff Hall Design
Photos by David Schalliol

3-10/.5M/jhdesign

Consortium on Chicago School Research

Directors

Penny Bender Sebring
Interim Co-Executive Director
Founding Co-Director
Consortium on Chicago School Research

Elaine M. Allensworth
Interim Co-Executive Director
Consortium on Chicago School Research

Melissa Roderick
Hermon Dunlap Smith Professor
School of Social Service Administration
University of Chicago

Steering Committee

Arie J. van der Ploeg, *Co-Chair*
Learning Point Associates

Steve Zemelman, *Co-Chair*
Illinois Network of Charter Schools

Institutional Members

Clarice Berry
Chicago Principals and Administrators Association

Barbara J. Eason-Watkins
Chicago Public Schools

Sarah Kremsner
Chicago Public Schools

Marilyn Stewart
Chicago Teachers Union

Steve L. Washington
Chicago Board of Education

Connie Wise
Illinois State Board of Education

Individual Members

Veronica Anderson
Stanford University

Carolyn Epps
Chicago Public Schools

Cornelia Grumman
Ounce of Prevention

Timothy Knowles
Urban Education Institute

Janet Knupp
Chicago Public Education Fund

Dennis Lacewell
Urban Prep Charter Academy for Young Men

Lila Leff
Umoja Student Development Corporation

Peter Martinez
University of Illinois at Chicago

Ruanda Garth McCullough
Loyola University

Gregory Michie
Illinois State University

Brian Spittle
DePaul University

Matthew Stagner
Chapin Hall Center for Children

Amy Treadwell
Chicago New Teacher Center

Josie Yanguas
Illinois Resource Center

Kim Zalent
Business and Professional People for the Public Interest

Martha Zurita
Youth Connection Charter School

Our Mission

The Consortium on Chicago School Research (CCSR) at the University of Chicago conducts research of high technical quality that can inform and assess policy and practice in the Chicago Public Schools. We seek to expand communication among researchers, policymakers, and practitioners as we support the search for solutions to the problems of school reform. CCSR encourages the use of research in policy action and improvement of practice, but does not argue for particular policies or programs. Rather, we help to build capacity for school reform by identifying what matters for student success and school improvement, creating critical indicators to chart progress, and conducting theory-driven evaluation to identify how programs and policies are working.